Citrus
Pomeg

Linda Borg-Winstanley

ShieldCrest

© Copyright 2023 Linda Borg-Winstanley

All rights reserved.

This book shall not, by way of trade or otherwise, be lent, re-sold, hired out, or otherwise circulated without the prior consent of the copyright holder or the publisher in any form of binding or cover other than that in which it is published and without a similar condition including this condition being imposed on the subsequent purchaser. The use of its contents in any other media is also subject to the same conditions.

ISBN: 978-1-915657-49-7

A CIP catalogue record for this book
is available from the British Library

MMXXIII

Published by
ShieldCrest Publishing.
Boston, Lincs, PE20 3BT
England +44 (0)1296 695 588
www.shieldcrest.co.uk

For my grandmother

Caroline Pewtress

"A Woman without love for her origins is lost."

Elena Ferrante

Introduction

I have asked myself why did I feel the need to write. I guess when we write it is partly for ourselves and partly to share. It has also been suggested to me that I explain why I wanted to write this story, my story. Hopefully, it will in its way be self explanatory.

I didn't want the Maltese story to be a footnote. As much as I tried to unpick or unravel the story of my family in Malta it wasn't until I went on Ancestry and had a DNA test that the moment of transition started to unfold. To say something changed for me is perhaps an understatement.

It is a story about believing in yourself, trusting yourself, and your feelings and following your heart.

I knew somewhere deep inside me that I had a strong connection with my father before I knew he was my father. I felt somewhere deep inside that I had a sister before I knew I had a sister. I knew somewhere deep inside my family being in Malta had a strong and deep resonance for me.

It all became clear and it all unfolded. It hasn't been the easiest of journeys at times but it has made itself apparent from my dad, to my sister, and my biological grandfather.

What I have learned is to follow your heart, believe in yourself and trust your instincts.

I feel at home.

One
Wiehed

I remember sitting on the sofa with my Dad, in his flat in Manchester and he told me that he was born in Malta. In fact, he was born in Paola on 2nd July 1912.

I had never heard of Malta and I had only just met my Dad! Two new things in my life.

My father's family lived in Malta for some years, I believe, something to do with my grandfather being connected with the Navy in some way.

There was also a story in the family that my grandparents were in Malta because my grandmother Caroline had weak lungs and their doctor had suggested they move to a warmer climate. Maybe that was why they went! Maybe it was because my grandfather was in the Navy and therefore it was easy for them to go to Malta; maybe a combination of the two? I know it would have taken quite a long time by boat.

Caroline and John, my grandparents, travelled from Manchester in England with their eldest son Jim who was quite young at the time. Jim was born 25th September 1901 in Manchester. Their second son George was also born in Manchester on 3rd July 1903 and records show that George was baptized on 12th August 1903 in Bradford, Lancashire.

My grandfather was working as an Engine Fitter at Devonport in the Dockyard at Plymouth before the family left for Malta. George sadly died whilst they were living in Devonport when he was only five months old and his death certificate shows that he died from Acute Gastritis. His death certificate also indicates that his father, my grandfather, was with George when he died on 24th December 1903. Maybe my grandmother was there too.

There were a lot of infant deaths around at the time unfortunately, mainly due to the fact that there weren't any antibiotics available. What it must have been like for my grandmother and grandfather to lose their child and for parents in general I will never know.

I was told by my aunt who was born in the middle of six brothers, that two of her brothers, George and Robert, both died when very young. George, she thought, while her parents were on their way to Malta and Robert, not long after they had arrived there. Indeed, my grandparents did lose their third son Robert not long after arriving and settling in Malta. Robert's death certificate, obtained from Malta, indicates that he was fourteen months old when he died at 2.30 am 1st August 1906 from Gastro Enteritis at home in Paola. He was buried in Bighi Cemetery, a Royal Naval Cemetery, in Paola.

Having researched some of the family history and finding documentation that confirms my grandparents did lose two sons fills me with a deep sadness, especially for my grandmother with whom I have always felt a closeness.

My dad told me that his father, my grandad, was a diver in Malta and that he was blown up whilst diving for diamonds but I don't think that was the real story or even the correct one.

My Aunt Ruby Melita, Leta as we knew her, told me that they came to England because my grandmother Caroline missed her family and it was something to do with the war. They came to England not long after the end of the first world war. I don't know the story or even the real reason and I guess I will never know.

Caroline and her five children returned to England around 1920 and her husband, my grandfather John, apparently returned five years earlier in 1915. According to his naval records he went to Devonport which was the naval base in Plymouth and from there to Scotland. But I am getting ahead of myself with the story.

As I said my grandmother and grandfather went to Malta and lived there with their son Jim, James Abraham. I don't actually know where they lived for all the time that they were there. They did live in Palma Street in Paola at one time. I have no idea whether they lived there all of the time. My dad did mention Valletta but I have been unable to get clarification to this very day. I guess it must have been somewhere near to the naval base. Paola is where the ships were and where my grandfather would have worked as a ships engineer.

In Paola Caroline and John's only daughter Leta was born on 13th April 1908 followed by their fourth son William Frederick, known as Bill, born on 4th August 1909. Then my father Bert, Herbert on his birth certificate, followed his siblings on 2nd July 1912. And after that the youngest member of the family, another son Thomas, again born in Paola, joined them all on 28th September 1915. He was always known as Tom or Tommy within the family.

By all accounts and all the stories and records my grandmother must have been in Malta for about twenty years.

I was told that my father was eight years old when the family came to England. My Aunt Leta being a little older was twelve. She told me that she thought her parents were totally mad coming to England from a warm country where the sun shone and the skies were blue, to a cold wet damp climate and as if that wasn't enough, to the damp greyness of Manchester. Manchester is known for its rain. In Malta she was used to walking to school in a dress in the warmth of the sunshine with blue skies, picking citrus fruit and or pomegranates on the way.

Citrus Fruit and Pomegranates

One of the stories my dad told me was that he had never seen snow before he came to England. He didn't know what snow was. It's hard to believe these days especially with our ability to connect so easily with other countries around the world. Social media today certainly has its advantages. As a boy he was out somewhere playing and it started snowing. He saw all this white stuff falling down from the sky and was really frightened because he didn't know what it was and thought it was going to cover him. He ran and knocked on the door of a nearby house. Apparently, the people who lived there were quite caring and understood that he was scared. They were kind enough to take him safely home to his family.

After my father passed in 1991, I decided it was time to go to Malta to see the country where my dad was born and where my family actually lived for all those years. It was quite exciting for me and I knew somewhere deep inside that I was searching for my roots.

The flight to Malta from England is quite a short flight which takes about three and a half hours. The change in temperature on the plane was quite amazing but not as amazing as the warmth that hit me when the door of the plane opened. It was an all-encompassing warmth like having a warm and cozy blanket wrapped around you. I was about to set foot on the land where my family once lived and where my father and my aunt and uncles were born. I felt both intrigued and excited at the same time. As the plane started its descent into Luqa airport to my surprise tears started to well up and roll down my cheeks? Why? Why on earth were tears rolling down my cheeks? Why did I feel so emotional?

Yes, I knew that my family lived in this country but they also lived in England, the same country where I lived. What on earth was going on? The family lived in Manchester and visiting the family home of Manchester doesn't seem to have that effect although it does hold some warmth for me. Maybe, it was due to the first-time visiting Malta and because that's where my dad was born. Maybe it was because he and my aunt had told me stories of this country where they spent the early part of their life. Not just a three and a half hour flight away but a long journey by boat. I wonder how long it took them to sail from Malta to England?

The warmth of Malta was stunning. The smell of the land seemed familiar to me. It felt as if I had always known this country somewhere deep inside of me and I felt immediately at home, as if I belonged.

For my first visit I stayed in Gozo, a small island just off the coast of Malta. I cannot recall why I made this choice at the time but it was quite easy to travel between Gozo and Malta. There was (and possibly still is) a regular and efficient ferry service and a regular and efficient bus service. Buses were at the time green in Gozo and yellow and orange in Malta. They were rather rickety and trundled slowly and happily to wherever you wanted to go, zig zagging the length and breadth of these two small islands.

The buses were privately owned by the bus drivers and personalised by them. They looked after their buses, cleaned them well and polished them to such a high standard you could see your reflection in the chrome. With Malta being a mainly Catholic country, the bus driver usually had a personalized altar on the bus which was a form both of protection and appreciation. Buses rumbled across the island in a leisurely fashion as if there was no hurry and no care in the world, knowing that we would reach our destination eventually.

There was and still is a very large bus terminal in Malta just outside the City Gate of Valletta, named Porta Reale. It somehow seemed huge to me then. The surrounding area of the terminal with its curved pavements was crowded and bustlng with people, Maltese and tourists. It had lots of kiosks selling snacks and cakes, cigarettes, newspapers, magazines, souvenirs and always bottled water which is always needed in such a warm climate. The buses seemed to move faster in the terminal than they did trundling to the required destination on the road. They circled round the large Tritons Fountain (completed in 1959) and you certainly had to keep a keen eye in the terminal as to where the buses were and where they were going to park up. Alongside this circular terminal and keeping an eye on the buses, you also needed to keep an eye out on the road inside the terminal as the buses came in and went out because the road was slippery at times with oil due to the heat. Many a person went a cropper.

When I first went to Malta I went by bus and then by ferry to Gozo. It seems very odd to say but the land and the country itself actually had a smell similar to that of my father. Gozo had a warm peaceful quiet feel to it or it certainly did when I first visited. My partner and I rented an apartment in Zlendi.

Having journeyed to Malta by ferry and bus, I was just outside the capital Valletta and in awe of its beauty. I was wondering where my grandparents might have lived with my father and his brothers and sister. The city was intriguing with its stunning architecture and narrow streets. Arriving in Valletta is something to be believed as it has quite an exceptional energy. All the crowded streets slope, either downhill or uphill depending on your orientation. The people in Valletta somehow seem to have lived there forever.

They were both warm and friendly and on a number of occasions I was actually mistaken for being Maltese which was rather a surprise to me. I explained quite a few times that I was English which was also met with some surprise. A lovely elderly gentleman in a newsagent shop in one of the side streets which are more like corridors than streets, was quite insistent that I was someone he knew from a nearby village. He spoke to me initially in Maltese and when I replied in English, he seemed quite perplexed. After we talked for a little while he told me that I was actually the image of someone he knew who lived in a village not too far away. He did say which village it was but I was so shocked at the time that I can't remember which village that he actually mentioned.

The bus terminal with its amazing fountain and the equally amazing Phoenicia hotel seemed to sit in some sort of magnitude graciously overseeing Malta. From Valletta all seems to slope downwards. If you travel from Sliema to Valletta by ferry everything goes uphill at a very steep pace. Steep upwards and downwards streets which are incredibly slippery. No wonder Vincent Vella called his book a Maltese odyssey "Slippery Steps".

My second trip to Malta, which was to become one of many visits, took me to a hotel in Gzira very near to Sliema more or less on the Sliema seafront promenade which gives exceptional views of the harbour and the famous fortifications of Valletta. From the hotel it was a short walk to the ferry which crossed the harbour to Valletta. For me the view of Valletta from the ferry was absolutely breath taking. Seeing Valletta in the distance towering over the sea in all its magnitude and grandeur with stored memories of times gone by was quite an overwhelming sight. It felt as though my ancestors were there, somewhere in the shadows, with their own memories and their own stories.

There are many boat tours with tour guides in Sliema ready take you round the island should you want to explore in that way. Also, Gzira, and Sliema have a convenient bus service to Valletta.

Obviously, with the passage of time a lot of changes had taken place but there was still a warmth and generosity with the people of this Mediterranean country that sits on the same latitude as Africa.

I bought everything I could as souvenirs: tea towels, lighters, bookmarks, tee shirts, key rings and mouse mats all embellished with Malta. I was so excited and so thrilled it was as if I had acquired something of my family.

When asked on occasions if this was my first visit, I proudly answered no and that I had been before and that my father was born in Malta. I still looked around and looked at people wondering why my father resembled them or how and why they resembled my father. I put the thoughts to bed with the warm satisfaction that they did, and I did, and that was just how it was. But did I put the thoughts to bed? There was still a mystery somewhere.

In one shop in Valletta a women working there explained to me that many years ago the first-born daughter in a Maltese family was called Melita which was my aunt's name and actually means Malta.

My third visit brought with it a stay in the same hotel. The same walk to the same ferry across the harbour to Valletta and the same walks exploring Sliema, getting familiar with the area. Like Valletta the area had a feeling of being at home for me. On some occasions it would be a bus journey to Valletta and then another bus around the island exploring various sites and places.

At one time on another visit, I stayed in Msida which I thought to be rather slower and calmer than Valletta or Sliema although it has the University of Malta. The students seem to come and go with their thoughts in their studies and books under their arms. In the evenings whilst walking we saw families sitting outside their homes chatting in the cooler air of the evening.

I discovered a cafe which was to become a favourite of mine called The Busy Bee. It was obviously a favourite with many Maltese people as well as it was always crowded, often with large families celebrating something. The coffee was good and the cakes an absolute delight and very large. Very large and very Maltese. It amused me that my Auntie Leta used to have large cream cakes waiting for me on my arrival at her home when I visited her in north Manchester. Perhaps that was something that remained stored in her memory along with the citrus fruit and pomegranates.

The fruit in Malta is beyond belief compared to England. It is usually large (like the cakes) and tastes absolutely delicious. I think it is due to the fact that it blossoms and ripens in the Mediterranean sun. The locally grown vegetables also have more flavour and they taste delicious along with Kinnie, a local drink made from oranges and herbs and Cisk, the excellent local lager.

Over the years I have stayed in various places including Valletta, Gzira, Sliema, Msida and Marsaxlokk and each time I visit I feel just as at home as the time before. On one occasion I was disappointed to learn that they were going to rebuild the beautiful Gate to Valletta but my fears were unfounded when I was fortunate enough to see the plans drawn up by the architect and the actual designs for the new Gate. Seeing it when it was actually built was as true as seeing the plans and that was a big relief. I did feel that something would be taken away with the old wall but it wasn't.

The Gate of Valletta whether old or new led me to the Agenda bookshop in Republic Street. I cannot remember or even grasp how many times I have visited there or how many books I have purchased whilst there. The books I do purchase are always by Maltese authors. One year I decided that the way forward was to purchase a Kindle which seemed to be very popular with various friends who had encouraged me. The Kindle had become very popular with folk especially when travelling. This apparently would cut down the need to buy so many books I was told and so I thought. It didn't. I like books and The Agenda bookshop got the better of me. I love that shop. I love bookshops in general. In fact, more than liking books, I love them.

There was another café as well as the Busy Bee which I really enjoyed visiting. It was rather small and was very popular with the Maltese locals. The people who worked in there were always friendly. It was always noisy. On most days there would be an enormous queue of people. They sold good coffee and various meals as well as Kinnie, Cisk and excellent pastizzi . Pastizzi is a traditional savoury pastry which has a filling of ricotta cheese or peas and to me the ones in this café were the best I had ever tasted. So, I visited quite frequently.

As it was always busy you were fortunate if you got a table but I learned to get the timing right so I was rarely disapointed. As well as being busy and noisy there was a huge television screen that outdid the size of the café. On one occasion, I heard an amazing voice above the noise and the hustle and bustle of the enthusiastic and talkative customers. The voice belonged to Andrea Bocelli. Obviously, this was quite a long time ago. I loved his voice. It was so powerful and moving. I was able to buy some of his C.Ds at the airport in Malta whilst waiting for my flight back to England. He became very well-known after this.

Sometimes you have to be quite swift at the airport because, being such a small island the planes are allocated a time slot and if the plane misses that slot for any reason, you can just sit on the plane and wait for what seems an age. It has happened. I have.

Two
Tnejn

I was born in February 1948 in Prestbury, Cheshire in a house that had at one time belonged to the fascist Oswald Mosley, unfortunately. Those of us who would have normally been born at the hospital in Manchester were actually born at this nursing home in Prestbury. It was due, I am told to the amount of bombing on Manchester during the second world war and many of the buildings had not been rebuilt or restored by then.

My mother wasn't the most maternal of women and she told me that she didn't really want children. She had lost a daughter before my arrival in the world. She did, apparently try a number of ways to abort me whilst she was pregnant but to no avail. The doctor friend she had spoken with about trying to terminate the pregnancy, well in fact me, told her that she had tried so many ways to abort that there was nothing else that could be done and the child obviously had a strong will for survival. So here I am.

My father was in the Lancashire Fusiliers and they were part of the Fourteenth Army who in 1944 and 1945 fought a brutal and gruelling war in the jungles of Burma which has since become Myanmar. The soldiers fought jungle warfare in the rainy season for which they were ill trained, ill prepared and ill equipped. It is thought that about 12,621 soldiers died during the Burma campaign. It was a campaign apparently overlooked by the press and remained far more obscure than the reporting of the war in Europe. These soldiers didn't return home in June 1945 when the Second World War was officially declared over. They returned to England in the August.

When my father did return home, he was so traumatized by his experience that he had to undergo electric shock treatment (ECT) to dispel the atrocities he had experienced. My mother had to keep him in a darkened room for either a twenty-four-hour or a forty-eight-hour period after one of these sessions without any keys or any sharp objects. Apparently, they didn't know what my father had experienced or what had happened to him and I am sure to many others similar to him.

These days when soldiers have experienced trauma in the war it is known as Post Traumatic Stress Disorder (PTSD) and they are offered some sort of support. Personally, I am not sure what sort of support this is or whether the support is actually of any benefit to the soldiers. For me and what I saw with my father the treatment offered is a type of band aid. It might cover over the surface and the cracks but it doesn't go to any depth to help eradicate the atrocities of war on an emotional level either immediately or even in the days that follow. Neither are soldiers given support or helped with how to re-adjust to life as a civilian.

I think it would be good to follow the same example as the Japanese after the Second World War. Since then, the Japanese have not engaged in warfare. I hold no judgement as both sides had their casualties and both sides had their friends and families. Mothers see their sons go to war. Wives see their husbands go to war. Sisters see their brothers go to war and so on. As the song, Mothers Daughters Wives by Judy Small states, 'The first time it was fathers the last time it was sons and in between your husbands marched away with drums and guns. It's not only men in uniform that pay the price of war'. Wars always have their casualties. We might wonder why we have war. In the words of Leonard Cohen in his song , 'Anthem' he sings 'and the wars they will be fought again'. Unfortunately, they are.

I remember as a child I was told on no account should a knife be left lying on a kitchen top or on a table and if there were any scissors around, they should be closed. One day I caught my father's eye and he was in a type of trance staring in a direction with perspiration like small beads swelling up on his forehead. I followed the direction of his gaze to a pair of scissors which were slightly open on the table. I was very young at the time and slowly and without much movement I placed my hand over the scissors to close them and also remove them from the table. My father stood there for a while and then it was as if he came back into his body and into present time from wherever he was and from whatever the situation. To this day I always move knives and close scissors. Some things always stay with you.

My mother left my father and left me with my father shortly after I was born. I was told that I was about two months old. She went to London to live with Mike. She took on Mike's last name rather than her married name of Winstanley and that was the name she became known by for the rest of her life. People have their reasons for what they do and people have their stories to which we have no entry.

My dad, so I am told looked after me for about the first eighteen months of my life. He used to have me with him in my pram whilst he worked in my aunt's garage so my aunt told me. She was going to help my dad bring me up. Then for some reason known only to my mother, she collected me from my father in Manchester and took me to London to live with her and Mike. Mike unfortunately became very ill not long afterwards. He developed lung cancer and the company he worked for found us somewhere to live in the Midlands, moving him, my mother and myself so he could have treatment at the Queen Elizabeth Hospital, which was the best hospital at the time for the treatment of cancer patients. It probably still is.

Mike died when he was forty-two. I was five. Apparently, I had become quite close to him and I remember him as a tall dark-haired man who used to wear a dicky bow. I also remember him laughing a lot, in fact I remember laughing a lot with him as we sat at the dining room table until he became really ill. I remember him in a stylish navy-blue dressing gown with white polka dots on it, I think they were fashionable at the time. He had a London accent and apparently so did I. He insisted on taking my mother and myself on holiday as he knew he wasn't long for this world. It was a kind and noble gesture but actually, he was far too ill to undertake such a task.

I remember him driving propped up with pillows and being very nauseous. One night at the hotel, he haemorrhaged. I remember a special train was arranged to take him back to the Midlands and back to the hospital. My mother didn't drive and was stranded at the hotel on the south coast with both myself and the car. Her common law husband had been taken away seriously ill and she wasn't with him. The man who owned the hotel we were staying in was kind enough to drive the car and us back home.

Consequently, with all that my mother went through and with Mike dying she had a nervous breakdown and was hospitalized. Apparently, she was pregnant at the time with a son. The powers that be thought the best thing for my mother was to abort the baby. A son who would have been my brother. My mother lost both her partner and their son which must have been tragic.

I grew up believing that Mike was my father and there was no reason for me to believe otherwise. Like my mother I shared Mikes last name although she never legally changed either of our names.

One lunch time when I was five years old and home from school, actually I was at a neighbour's for my lunch and she told me that my daddy had died. I asked what that meant and she said that I would never see him again. I remember feeling very sad. At the time I had three friends who were children of neighbours. We were all of a similar age, John, Brian and Michael. John's family were Catholic and he explained to me that when someone dies, they go onto different planes. John and I would stand in the garden together looking up at various planes as they flew overhead waving and wondering whether Mike might be on it.

When I was eleven years old, I needed my birth certificate to take to my new school. My mother delayed in giving it to me, in fact she was quite reticent. One day I told her that I was getting into trouble at school and that I really needed to take my birth certificate in. My mother then said she needed to talk to me. It transpired that the name on my birth certificate wasn't the name that I was known by. Obviously, I was curious. I asked why my name was different on my birth certificate and then my mother told me that Mike wasn't my father. I was shocked. I was also quite confused and perplexed. I asked her who my father was and she told me it was the person that I knew as my uncle Bert. My dear uncle Bert, the man I felt so very close to. The man I never wanted to leave whenever we visited Manchester. The man who always asked us to stay and my mother always said no and I always cried and said I wanted to stay with him. I always got dragged away sometimes in tears. This was the man I used to live with. This was my birth DAD! No wonder I had a strong bond with him and always felt so close to him.

Why didn't my dad keep me? Why did I have to live with my mother who didn't seem to particularly want me anyway? When you are eleven and when you have received such a bombshell as this you have no idea and no clue what to do with your emotions. I'm not sure whether it was the information I had just received or the lack of truth that caused my confusion and consequently my withdrawal. Possibly a bit of both. My mother gave me my birth certificate in an envelope with the name of the school secretary on it. Inside was an explanation letter. It was to be given to the secretary directly, so that none of my friends would see that my name was different to the one they knew me by and consequently no questions would be asked of me.

I guess I withdrew to try and make sense and understand why no one had ever told me the truth? I wondered why I was with my mother? Why wasn't I with my Dad? Why had everyone colluded with the story that Mike was my father? Did anyone actually know that Mike wasn't my father? As my mother had moved from Manchester to London and then to the Midlands perhaps no one knew. My life became quieter and even more insular. At the time I felt cheated by both my mother and by my dad and withdrew into my own isolated world. Sometimes words are totally inadequate and explanations are not quite enough.

The same evening I was given the information about my father my mother went out and I took the opportunity to search the house. I rummaged around until I found a tin box in her dresser with some papers and certificates in. There, in this blue tin, was a pink and black birth certificate with my name on it and in black ink, it stated, father Herbert Winstanley and mother Hilda Winstanley. A certificate with information of my own unexamined past. That was that. Job done. It was true they were my parents and my name was Linda Winstanley.

Not long after starting my senior school which was one of the newly built comprehensives, they thought I should sit the entrance exam for the local grammar school. They were quite confident that I would pass and be able to transfer. King Edwards was believed to give you a better education than the school I was at. You could become a professional at something by going on to university and then on to something else, whatever that something else might be. I didn't want to take the entrance exam so I didn't and, in hindsight, whether this was the right decision or not I don't really know. It was at the time. I didn't want to leave the friends I had made and I certainly didn't want to start on another journey for which I felt ill equipped. I had had enough of journeys to last me a life time. Manchester, London, the Midlands. Father no Mother. Mother new Father. No Father no Mother. When Mike died and my Mother was hospitalized, she was absent, for quite a while due to her breakdown. She stayed absent on and off after that but then she was always absent on and off beforehand.

I decided that I was staying put at my comprehensive school with my friends. My friends were solid and they were my friends no matter what. We studied together, in a fashion. We played sport together which fortunately I was good at. I also liked people so I got on well with most of the other pupils and the teachers. Maybe it was because I was friendly and good at sports that I was voted to be the House Captain. A position voted for by the pupils and backed by the staff, a type of merit position rather than that of a prefect which was a position elected solely by the staff.

On my first day at my new comphrehensive school, we played rounders in the afternoon. I think it was a bonding exercise beacuse the whole of the new first year was involved. We were playing rounders and I managed to catch the games teacher out. She announced to us all in good humour that it was a fluke and said that she was taking it again. I caught her out the second time. She then announced that from that moment on I was going to be on her team while I remained at school. We all laughed. I felt safe and I was having fun so I wasn't going anywhere. I loved quite a few subjects at school in particular English, Music, Physiology, Drama and Sport.

The reason I didn't actually go to a grammar school in the first place was because I needed two eye operations as a child. Overall, I lost twelve weeks schooling and consequently went from an A Stream to a B Stream. I became what was known as cross eyed through shock. Maybe it was a culmination of things in my early life. Maybe it was the shock of being left with strangers when Mike died. No one came to collect me from the nursery that night so I had to sleep there. The nursery was run by quite an unpleasant woman who not only bit me on one occasion but also hit me. I remember the morning after spending the night there I was very unwell and I was holding on to the bannister rail because I could neither walk nor talk. The woman whose house it was and ran the nursery was shouting at me and hitting me and apparently telling me to move. Fortunately, another woman who worked at the nursery arrived and as she looked up the stairs and saw what was happening shouted at her to stop and said couldn't she see that I was ill. She ran up the stairs, picked me up and hugged me. I was ill. The shock of everything had caused me to lose the use of my legs. I went cross eyed as mentioned and apparently my brain closed down.

The woman who rescued me and picked me up and hugged me took me home to her house. She was my guardian angel for the rest of her life and I guess in a way became my surrogate mother. In later years I stayed with her during the school holidays and at weekends. She was the person who visted me when I was hospitalised. Her daughter and I also became close. She was a few years older than me and behaved as if she was my older sister. She used to let me tag along with her and her friends when they went out and even when they met boys. Mainly with bicycles and cycling in the park at the time. I was always very pleased to be included and we always had a good time together. Like most siblings she and I also had times of arguing and fighting, but we always sorted it out and we always remained close.

When I was eight years old, I moved to a different school in the Midlands. The Head of the school only allowed the A stream students to sit the 11+ which was the entrance exam to a grammar school. Consequently, I didn't sit this exam due to being in the B stream. The Head wanted a hundred percent pass rate for the school so that it looked good.

The comprehensive school that I went to was so enormous that we frequently got lost. Each floor looked the same and all the corridors looked the same, mainly because they were. I turned up at school on the first day of my new life and stood in this extremely large hall along with many other anxious eleven-year-old children, all looking clean and neat in our pristine new uniform (which I disliked). They were bottle green. There must have been at least a hundred and fifty of us all nervously assembled together.

The way of allocating the students to their allotted class was far from a scientific process or even an educational process as far as I am aware. There were five streams 1E1, 1E2, 1-1, 1-2 and 1-3. We were allocated to a class in alphabetical order. The allocation was that someone by the name of Allsop would go into 1E1. Then Atkins into 1E2. Followed by Bailey into 1-1 Davies to 1-2 and Edwards to 1-3 - Fellows to 1E1 and so the process went on until everyone had a class. 1E1 and 1E2 were apparently GCE classes. My last name at the time began with a D and I was allocated the class of 1-1, apparently a commercial class. I am unsure regarding the other two classes, maybe they were the same or maybe they were classes that were not examination classes. I don't really remember. We girls in 1-1 were destined to go on to do shorthand and typing and the boys technical drawing and woodwork. This certainly wasn't apparent to us in the first year. In fact the first couple of years were great until the realization of becoming a secretary dawned on me and it certainly wasn't my life plan. I went to see the Head of the school and asked him if I could transfer to one of the other classes and take my O-Levels but he explained that there were too many in both of those classes already but he would see what he could do. He didn't do anything.

My teachers were again very supportive and suggested that I should try and go on to teacher training college. Because of one thing and another, that didn't happen and being in a commercial class didn't help either. My mother also said that she couldn't keep me anymore and that really I needed to go out and get a job and bring some money into the house. Actually, it was a flat.

I didn't really enjoy shorthand and typing, and I certainly didn't want to be a secretary. I quite liked the shorthand bit because I used to imagine that we were spies in a foreign country with access to a secret code which needed to be cracked. I was in fact good at codes and my mother's friends used to ask me to play the one arm bandits for them at their club until I was banned. I was banned because I managed to work out the sequence of the codes and therefore how to win the jackpot! The people who ran the club decided enough was enough and I was banned and disappointed. The typing was fun when we all had to tip tap on the keys in rhythm together and there was a loud PING from the typewriters as we came to the end of the line. It always caused a giggle in the classroom. I learnt touch typing which has been a bonus throughout my life with both typewriters and then computers.

Linda Borg-Winstanley

I always loved English and I have always loved reading. I loved books and stories that would transport me to places I had never imagined. Reading was an escape from reality. I would go home and devour whatever book we had been assigned at school and then had to endure patiently (or impatiently) wading through it in class, which was rather like having ongoing toothache as far as I was concerned. It was during my fourth year that I developed a love for Shakespeare, much to the delight of my English teachers.

I exasperated my needlework teacher, and she thought that the best place for me was in the library rather than having to put up with my laborious efforts in the needlework class. It was absolutely fine by me. I could read whatever books I wanted. I loved the library, and I loved being in there on my own with all these books in a variety of colours, in different shapes and sizes and with their own particular smell. Just sitting quietly by the window reading whatever I had chosen and escaping from reality, I was in my element. When we had a dissection session in a science lessons, I was once again directed to the library rather than the teacher having to cope with me passing out. More books and more reading what else could I have asked for. The privacy of being on my own, either working or reading in a library, is something I continue to appreciate to this day.

When I was in the fourth year, I did spend quite a bit of time truanting from school. It was the year that shorthand and typing and commerce reared their head. I didn't want to do shorthand or typing but I was interested in commerce and the world of business. I think overall, I was bored and under functioning. I was spending time trying to be engaged and interested in subjects that didn't hold any interest for me. I decided there was no point being at school, for the rest of the day sitting through endless hours of tedium listening to information about things that held no interest. I went to school and was there for registration and marked present. It was assumed that I was in school for the rest of the day and no questions would be asked so I would wander off home. There was no one at home and I had a door key.

My parents Bert and Hilda had been married for twelve years when I was born, I believe that they were quite in love with each other. When my mother first saw my father, it was at a dance hall in Manchester. She went with a friend and saw my dad through the glass door. He was having fun and dancing with a male friend. My mother said to her friend that she was going to marry him. Her friend told her not to be silly because she didn't know him. At the time my father was a professional ballroom dancer and as the story goes, one day, he asked my mother if she would be interested in being his dance partner. His current dance partner was going to be married and was emigrating to Australia. She accepted the offer and became his dance partner and then his wife. They were professional ballroom dance partners. For some reason everyone had always told my mother that my dad would never propose. However, they were in a competition one time and dancing a Tango when my father asked my mother if she would marry him. She was so astounded that she stopped on the dance floor and consequently they were disqualified but they did get married. Like so many couples at the time the war intervened and wove its own story.

When I was young, probably about ten years old, I was a given a beautiful candle at Christmastime. It had wax that resembled icing on the outside and it was pink on the inside. When it was lit It glowed and emanated a pink hue. It was extremely unusual. I thought that it was absolutely wonderful, it seemed like magic to me at the time. Along with this candle I was given three white cotton handkerchiefs with an embroidered Brownie in the corner, each in a different colour. Dark brown, light brown and a mustard colour. I was a happy Brownie. They, like the candle were extremely unusual and I was as impressed with the handkerchiefs as I was with the candle. They were just beyond the normal sort of gift.

For my fourteenth birthday I was allowed and excited to have a party at home and as we had a very large front room, I was able to invite quite a few friends. We all felt so very grown up. During the party a man came in with my mother and he gave me an unusual birthday present which I thought was extremely kind of him as I didn't really know him. It was a plastic folder in which you were able to keep your records which were predominantly 45's at the time. The cover was white with brightly coloured people dancing on it. If my memory serves me correctly, they were rock and rolling or jiving I think the term was then. Apparently, this was the same man who had given me the candles and handkerchiefs when I was ten years old, but I didn't know then who he was.

I didn't know who he was, and I didn't know at this point that he and my mother were lovers or that he would become an important figure in my life. He, David became more or less my stepfather and although he and my mother never married, he shaped my life in many ways.

David taught me among other things to think and appreciate art, to be able to question and debate. To appreciate good cars, to enjoy a good book, to appreciate good food and to drink and appreciate good brandy. I believe as I got older, I inherited from him a dislike for library books and a dislike for badly printed books. It felt like there was something more personal and private with your own book, as if it held some kind of magic. David was different to both my father and Mike, who were both quite tall and dark. David was smaller about five foot nine. And my dad and Mike were about five foot eleven to six foot. According to my mother he wasn't a dancer either. He was a very well-educated man who had a background as a printer and went on to have his own business printing books. He had studied at Harvard and at one time been a Brigadier General in the army.

When I was sixteen, I went on holiday with my mother to Jersey for some reason. We hadn't been on holiday together since I was a child, I don't really know why we went. Anyway, we did, and we had a really good time. We met up with various people and we often travelled around the island together in the daytime and then met with them again in the evenings. I met Joseph who was from Sardinia, he was quite a lot of fun and a really good dancer. We danced away the nights to Herb Alpert and the Tijuana Brass who were very popular in the sixties. I felt so very grown up.

Sean the night porter at the hotel we were staying at in Jersey, apparently, called the police late one night saying that he had been knocked unconscious by someone who had robbed the hotel safe and had taken all the money. Unfortunately, for Sean the bump on his head and the timing in regaining consciousness didn't quite add up as far as the police were concerned. They found the money in the post box just outside the hotel in an envelope addressed to Sean's family, he was arrested and taken off to the police station. At the time I was excited about the drama of the occasion but also disappointed that I wouldn't see Sean again. I had quite a crush on him as well as Joseph but then I was sixteen.

I hadn't really spoken with my father or had that much contact with him in recent years probably since the episode regarding my birth certificate. I think I was possibly harbouring some deep-seated grief about not being with him. I'm not totally sure what it was. I was young. He always phoned me on a Tuesday evening at ten past seven, usually on his way to wherever he went, probably dancing. It was before he had a phone installed at home and when he did have his phone installed mainly to stop me nagging him, he continued to call me on a Tuesday evening at ten past seven. He was an extremely punctual man by nature. As I recall he always sent me gifts throughout my life which were accompanied with a letter. When he had the phone installed, I was really pleased as I could call him anytime and check in for a chat and see how he was. Also, I could call and suggest I popped in for a visit which was always okay and always seemed to please him.

It was a strange time and whilst we were in Jersey there was a song often played on the radio by Chuck Berry mentioning someone named Marie. My mother disliked this song with an intensity and a passion that was very unlike her. I didn't know why it upset her so much and I was concerned whenever it came on the radio.

Whilst in Jersey I decided for some reason to send my father a post card. It seemed like something I really wanted to do and a nice thing to do at the time, so I did. To my surprise when I returned home to England there was a letter waiting for me from my father saying how pleased he was to receive my card. I cried and wept for the loss.

Also, not long after we had returned home, we received a phone call from my uncle, my mother's brother, to say that his wife, my aunt, had died. I didn't know her; I am not sure whether my mother and uncle were even speaking with each other at the time. They hadn't spoken with each other for something like sixteen years. Another surprise for me and another unknown family member entered my life. I went with my mother to Manchester to my aunt's funeral. I didn't know many people there. I got to know my uncle and met my cousin. He is my only cousin on my mother's side, I was amused as he was about six foot six and I am five foot two. I think it must have been a time of healing for my mother and her brother because he used to stay with us quite a lot after that. Also, we used to visit him and sometimes I would go and stay with him on my own and sometimes with a friend. My uncle eventually remarried and there became a closeness that wasn't there previously within my mother's side of the family.

After my aunt's funeral and before catching the train back to Birmingham my mother and my dad had arranged for the three of us to meet. I remember being very excited and very nervous at the same time. I was excited at the prospect of seeing my dad. He had told me on the phone that he wouldn't be going to the funeral as he didn't like funerals. I wondered if any one did. We were waiting for him near the station and standing on the pavement which is rather like a ramp leading up to Piccadilly Station. There were crowds of people walking towards the station when my mother pointed to a man in the crowd walking in our direction. That's him she said. That was my dad and when I asked how she knew from such a distance she said that she would recognize his walk anywhere. I guess it might have had something to do with them both having been professional dancers and dance partners at that. I did see them dance together on one or two occasions and I must admit they were quite exceptional. I thought that they were like film stars. Everyone was cheering and clapping them. My father had apparently been a judge at one time and worked with Victor Sylvester. I learnt that you needed to be a pretty good dancer to become a judge.

So, there we were the three of us sitting in a pub, my biological parents and me. The three of us together. I remember that they talked with each other quite a lot. It felt very strange. I felt very strange. It was as if I was in some sort of bubble that seemed to have floated upwards towards the ceiling and was watching the proceedings from above. In no time we were back on the train again to Birmingham. After that I used to go and visit my dad on a regular basis and got to know him.

Then somehow, I arranged to go and visit him in Manchester on my own and stay overnight. It was exciting to think that I would have time with my dad. I remember very little about it apart from going dancing with him. I remember being asked on several occasions if I was a good dancer like my mother and father. The answer was no. If I remember correctly, I went with friends to ballroom dancing classes about three times in my life. I think it was Victor Sylvester's School of Dancing. I was pleased to eventually pluck up the courage to have a waltz with my dad (so was he) I was also pleased when he said that I was a good dancer.

I can't remember whether I stayed with my dad on more than one occasion or not. One Saturday on my return home and I use the term loosely as it never really felt like a home, as I never felt safe, my mother asked what my dad was doing that afternoon and I told her that after seeing me onto the train to Birmingham, he was getting a train to Stockport and going to a wedding. She was standing in the kitchen and said, without even a glance in my direction, that it was the wedding of his other daughter. I walked away. I walked to my bedroom and closed the door. I couldn't assimilate any more information. I had just returned from seeing my dad and I couldn't take in any more information especially regarding my family. Finding out about my father was enough. Fathers and now sisters. My mother and I never spoke about it again. I never spoke with my dad about it either. I'm sure my mother was extremely disturbed by whatever had happened with my father and that he had another daughter. Retrospectively, I wish we had had a conversation but at the time I was going through my own emotions.

Years later after my dad had died, I found out that my father's other daughter (my sister) had the name Marie in her name, I think that is why my mother hated the song so much when we were in Jersey. She must have married when I was about eighteen, I remember because it was around the time when I first stayed with my dad that he went on to the wedding. What on earth was the story? My mother had obviously known about her. Is this what drove my parents apart?

After both of my parents had died, I spent quite a bit of time at Stockport library wading through micro fiche of old newspapers to see if I could ascertain when my sister had married and who she might be. I knew approximately when and where she married. Whilst carrying out this task I became friendly with one of the librarians. Barbara had worked for Barnardo's and had been involved in researching and tracing the children who were sent from England to Australia. We talked quite a bit, and she became interested in my story and helped me with my research, possibly because of her previous interest and expertise in tracing people. She also carried out some research for me between my visits.

One time when I arrived at the library, Barbara thought she had located who my sister might be and where she had lived with her mother and sister. The information was fascinating, and it looked as though she might have lived outside of England for a while. The exciting thing was that we did now have an address. I thought as I sat there in the library if I had driven to Stockport and if I had my car with me, I could drive to the house to see if I could get any information. I mentioned this to Barbara whilst we were chatting and looking at the documentation in front of us. Later on, during the morning Barbara said if I really wanted to go, she had her car and would drive me over in her lunch break. Bingo! I certainly did. So, without any hesitation I said, 'let's go and visit and check it out'. Barbara drove me. She kindly and patiently waited for me in her car just round the corner and left me to approach the house on my own.

I arrived and was warmly greeted and promptly invited into the house which was a surprise. The woman who opened the door to me and invited me in said, 'Hello love come in', as if she both knew me and was expecting me. I was rather surprised to say the least. There was also a younger woman there standing in the sitting room who was tall with dark hair. I explained to both of them that I was trying to locate a woman and explained who she was and that I believed at one time she had emigrated to Australia. I believed that she had lived at this address. They had a discussion between them and then the younger woman said that there was someone who had lived further down the road who was the builder's daughter who had emigrated to Australia. The mother questioned this, and after further discussion that appeared quite complicated between the two of them, I assumed that I must be with the wrong people and in the wrong house. They certainly didn't seem to know of this woman. I decided that it was best to leave apologizing for bothering them.

I went out to the car where Barbara was waiting and told her it was the wrong house and that they knew nothing of my sister. My friend immediately said that they were lying and that she had been in this business long enough to know that this was the right house with the right people. She drove me back to the library. Retrospectively, I wish she had come into the house with me. I was confused and disheartened.

At one time I had tried to obtain a copy of my sister's marriage certificate in Stockport, but I was told that there was no documentation and no record of the marriage. Consequently, on my return to Birmingham I phoned the record office in London to see if I could possibly locate a marriage certificate. The person I spoke with was exceedingly pleasant and said it would take about a week before I received the certificate but surprisingly enough it arrived the next morning. My heart was beating fast as I saw the envelope lying on the mat. I opened the envelope with some trepidation only to find that she had indeed got married from the very same house that I had visited the day before. To say that it was a surprise is an understatement. So, who were these people I visited and why didn't they tell me the truth? I was shocked. Why more secrets? Why not speak the truth and why was I constantly entangled in other people's secrets?

Over time I thought that I had tracked down my sister and I did write to her on two or three occasions, but it fell on stony ground and there was no response. I know she had her own reasons which I totally respect but for me I feel sad that she didn't want any contact. I have seen two of her sons who do look rather like my father.

Life continues in some shape or form and there are moments of transition, and in that transition something actually changes. After all, I had made contact with my dad, and I had developed a really good relationship with him. It was so easy and fell into place as if it always had been. I guess that's because it always had been. I went to Manchester to visit him regularly. I met his older brother Bill who was far from well as his lungs had been damaged, I believe due to asbestos in his past work environment. My grandmother had weak lungs too which probably didn't help Bill. I met uncle Bill and his wife Nellie, Uncle Tom and his wife Kath, and also, probably my favourite, my dad's sister, my auntie Leta. Maybe she was my favourite because she was my aunt and my dad's only sister or just because we had some sort of connection beyond relationship. She did tell me quite a bit of the family history. Of course, it could also have been because I spent time with her in my early childhood when my dad was at her house. She was going to help him bring me up after all.

Leta was always totally honest with me, with a sense of humour that was like my father's and apparently mine as well. I remember my mother saying to me, 'You have a sense of humour just like your fathers. I don't think it was meant as a compliment. My Dad's eldest brother Jim had retired and lived in Wales. He moved into a Home after his house was flooded and I didn't get to meet him until after my dad had passed away. My dad had asked me to go and see him and I did visit him a few times. Jim also had a lovely sense of humour. He told me that he was sitting in his house reading the newspaper and he could hear water bubbling away. He looked around and saw the water seeping into the room. I asked what he did, he said he rolled his trousers up, put his feet up and carried on reading the paper. He did lose his bungalow because of the flooding and moved into a Home where he spent the remainder of his life. I knew my dad would be pleased that I had visited him.

As no one except my mother had ever mentioned my dad having another daughter and I had not mentioned it to anyone either, I didn't know whether it was true, or not because it had never been spoken about by anyone else. After my dad had died and as I was sorting through his belongings, I came across quite a few photographs and amongst them were pictures of a young woman growing up over the years who did rather resemble my dad and there were also photographs of my dad at her wedding. I knew immediately that this was my sister. I just felt it. We always know such things instinctively. However, as she had never been mentioned by anyone ever apart from my mother, I decided that I would dispose of the photos. At the time I was staying with my godmother's daughter Wendy in Cheshire. Wendy's mother was my godmother, my mother was Wendy's godmother. Our parents had been very close friends and we had always been very close too. In the car driving back to Birmingham, my partner Rosi said she had something she wanted to tell me, it was that I had a sister. Wendy had told Rosi. My dad had apparently told my godmother.

I was out having lunch one time with my dad and my godmother in Cheshire, at a place called the Egerton Arms. Whilst we were there apparently, my dad told my godmother that he had another daughter and he wondered whether to tell me. My godmother thought it best that he didn't as she thought it would upset me. I understand why she thought this, I totally understand and respect her thoughts because she always always had my best interests at heart. With hindsight I wish that I had been told. At one time my godmother had spoken with Wendy about my dad having another daughter and they both decided they would tell me after my dad had passed. Unfortunately, my godmother died three weeks before my dad. Wendy was then left with the information about my sister and understandably didn't know whether to tell me or not so she spoke with Rosi who said she would tell me as she believed that I had a right to know.

In the car driving back to Birmingham I was told that I had a sister. I said that I knew. Knowing that having a sister was now a reality and not some figment of my mother's imagination gave me an inner sense of relief in a way. The woman in the photographs was in fact my father's daughter. She was my sister. The next morning, I phoned Wendy and asked her to take the photographs out of the dustbin, but she said that the binmen had been. The photographs were gone.

Around this time my friend spoke with my dad's brother, my Uncle Tom, and explained to him she had been told that my dad had another daughter. He said this was untrue and my dad didn't have another daughter. He stuck to this story for quite a while even when I asked him. He stood by the story even when my Aunt Leta suggested I asked him because she said he knew. He never spoke with me about it. Then one day out of the blue he gave me two photographs of the person I recognised from the wedding photographs to be my sister. More mystery. What on earth was the story and what was this secret?

All this explosion of information was going on between my dad passing and his funeral. The funeral was a very strange affair as I didn't know the majority of the people there. One of my cousin's partners asked who I was and when I said he was my dad she said she didn't know that my dad had a daughter. Had a daughter! He had two! I was concerned and wondered whether my sister was there? Was she actually at the funeral? If so, how would I know. In fact, would anybody know?

One evening quite a while later I decided to phone my Auntie Leta and ask her whether my dad actually had another daughter. She always spoke the truth and always, as they say, called a spade a spade. She said straight away that he had but she was living in Australia. She also said, 'You are not going to try and find her are you because she doesn't know that your dad is her dad'. My reply was, 'At least we have that in common'. Apparently, she returned from Australia to England the same year that my/our dad died. When my dad told my aunt about her, she had asked him if he was sure she was his daughter, his reply was yes, he was and that she was "the spit of him".

After my dad's death I continued to visit my Auntie Leta in north Manchester and often her granddaughter Gilly would be there as well. I was very fond of Leta. I also visited my uncle Tom and his wife Kath. My dad had four siblings, Jim was in Wales and Bill in Manchester, but I didn't really know any of my cousins or any other members of my father's family. I have one cousin on my mother's side, I don't really know him. I occasionally phone him and we exchange Christmas cards, but that is about it.

My father lived in Manchester, I lived approximately a hundred and twenty miles away in Birmingham. Not knowing my relatives when my dad passed was painful for me, I don't remember that much about the funeral. My uncle Tom's son, my cousin Tony and his partner Jean were kind enough to invite people back to their house for food and drinks after the funeral and also, I guess, to reminisce, which usually happens when someone has passed. I didn't really know many of the people there and I stuck quite closely by my Uncle Tom probably because I felt somewhat safe with my father's younger brother. I did feel rather like a stranger at my father's funeral.

Later that day I went back to stay with Wendy overnight rather than travelling back to Birmingham. I knew Wendy well and we had known each other forever. I felt safe with her as if she was my actual family. She knew my dad and my mum, and her parents and my parents as I said had been very close friends. Life continues and goes on and I guess we make the most of it and adapt to situations.

Eventually, I went on to get my degree. I read sociology. I enjoyed studying, debating and the discussions we had. It was far more interesting for me than my school days. Possibly because I had chosen the options that I was interested in and that obviously appealed to me.

I had worked in a couple of offices up until this point and then I was fortunate enough to be accepted for a post as an administrator/community worker within an organisation that was predominantly a night shelter for homeless young men between the ages of sixteen and twenty-five. The organisation ran training schemes for these young men and the one I was involved in taught woodwork and carpentry which I knew absolutely nothing about, but I did know how to organise and I really believed in the work of the organization. I loved working there and with the homeless lads seeing them learning a trade and developing faith in themselves. We had a good time. On the whole they were extremely bright and there were many reasons for them being homeless. The organization had hostels where the lads would move to after being at the night shelter and alongside learning a trade, they would be able to find employment and consequently earn some money to move on to having somewhere of their own to live. It was so rewarding when they said that they were able to hold their heads up and be proud and that they had personal integrity.

Whilst I was there, we went on residentials and took the lads sailing which was so much fun and we had many hilarious moments. On one occasion we were out at sea and two of the lads had forgotten to put the oars on the boat so when the engine failed, we were unable to row ashore. We did have a rendering from them of, "Oh we're going to Barbados" which was quite funny in a way. Les, who was the main sailor and the director of the organization managed eventually to get the boat ashore when the current was in our favour. He was very committed to working with young people. At one time he decided he would give up smoking and save the money he would spend on cigarettes and buy a sailing boat. He wanted to take the young people from the organisation on residentials and teach them how to sail. He did just that.

Prior to my degree I managed to obtain a couple of certificates, one in Community and Advice Work and another in Work with Women and Girls. It was because of these I was accepted on the degree course. For my placement year, I was fortunate enough to be involved in a course which was part of a university programme where I was able to both teach and do research. To this day I enjoy both. I like the solitude and intensity of research and the connection with people when teaching.

I was just about to start my Master's Degree when something else reared its head. I went to a graduation ceremony for Acupuncture students from the College of Traditional Acupuncture in Leamington Spa. It was something that changed my life. The staff spoke from their heart with such passion and belief about working with the body and spirit along with the mind. It was as if a switch went on inside me and the following day, I phoned the college for a prospectus.

It wasn't too long after that when I attended an Open Day and, sometime later, I enrolled on the course. Apart from loving every aspect of the course and work since, it is something that has afforded me a living now for thirty years. Eventually, I was fortunate enough to join the faculty at the college where I taught on the degree course for thirteen years. After that I taught at another Acupuncture Institution for another five years. During all this time I was in private practice. I feel quite blessed to be fortunate enough to have had such an experience.

Three
Tlieta

I think it was due to a conversation I was having with an old friend who was conducting her own family research. As we chatted, I became more and more interested and it was fascinating to hear about her family and where they actually lived, where they originated from initially and what she had found out about them during her research. We had been good friends for many years, we went way back having initially got to know each other through our interest in drama and being in the same theatre group. Because of our friendship her parents and my mother got to know each other quite well and they in turn became friends. Consequently, we all used to go out for evening meals together when my friend's parents were visiting her in Birmingham.

My friend also used to go to Manchester with me to visit my father. We would often have a meal with him and usually in a Chinese restaurant as she reminded me very recently. I think it was the location that appealed to us rather than the preference for Chinese food. The restaurant was in the centre of Manchester, we could meet there easily. Sometimes my friend and I would meet in the evening somewhere with my dad and his brother Tom for a drink and a chat. We would go and visit my dad in Manchester and occasionally we would visit my friend's parents at their home in Yorkshire. We constantly joked, and still often do, about each of us being from the wrong side of the Pennines. It is a very old joke to do with the War of the Roses. I'm not quite sure why we do this, I think it is a sort of friendship thing you might do with an old friend that you are close with for some reason. We were both involved in a drama group in Birmingham and some of our friends moved to Manchester to set up a theatre company there. We would often travel together to the Northwest on a Friday evening to see a production at the theatre. It was not only just the two of us but often three or four of us clambering into a car that we hoped would make the journey.

On occasions we used to travel to London to see a show, crammed into the same old rickety car which sometimes didn't make it due its age. Certainly, one time the car did break down, but we managed to make it to the theatre in time. We must have seen Jesus Christ Superstar at least three times. On one occasion we managed to book and pay for a box. I think the actual idea to have a box was so we could sing and dance along with the show. We had youth on our side. We thought it a much better idea than sitting in the stalls where you couldn't really move. Being static when the show was so vibrant with so much dancing and music was limiting for us to say the least. We loved the theatre. The night when we were in the box, we had been thoroughly enjoying ourselves dancing along at the end of the show the cast turned to our box and applauded and bowed. We were young, totally enthusiastic, and obviously not shy. We were pleased that the cast thought we were worth applauding. I think they might have enjoyed our enthusiasm as much as we enjoyed the show. The innocence of youth. We had rushed to London and to the theatre down the M1 motorway from our own play rehearsal in Birmingham and were absolutely full of enthusiasm.

Not all of us who used to go to Manchester met with my father, just one or two friends and of course my friend from the wrong side of the Pennines. I remember staying in Manchester one night after a show. We were staying at a friend's house and in the morning, I volunteered to pop out to the shop to get some milk and a newspaper. When I went outside, I knew exactly where I was due to my childhood and living in Manchester or even perhaps my adolescent memory of being in Manchester and staying with a relative. It was a very strange experience. It was an odd feeling not knowing where you are and at the same time knowing where you are. It was, however, quite a familiar feeling for me.

Alongside my friend's interest in tracing her family, my partner's brother had also developed an interest in tracing their family history and not only tracing family but having a DNA test. He was extremely interested in his family connections and where the family had originated from and chatted very enthusiastically about it all. The DNA test would apparently not only identify your family connections but also identify which country your ancestors would have lived in. It would highlight where your blood ties and blood line would have originated from alongside the percentage of the ethnicity. All very exciting and fascinating.

With my friend's story and my brother in law's interest having captured my interest I decided to take the plunge and look into my own family history. I joined Ancestry. Like so many people, I knew relatively nothing, some snippets perhaps. I had learnt some very basic information along the way when asking my mother, my dad and my aunt but all in all a relatively small amount. Some of us have become interested in our roots and making sense of who we are. We are interested in knowing where we come from and learning about our ancestors' stories. What's our parents' story? Whether we are brought up in our birth family and living with them or whether we are living with our adopted family it is important for some of us to know our roots. I guess in some way it helps to give us a sense of identity. Some of my friends and relations are not in the least bit interested in delving into their family story and possibly that's because they feel secure. Sometimes they just don't wish to know because they know enough information to satisfy themselves. For some who are adopted they don't want to look any further because they have had a happy adoption and don't want to upset the family who have adopted them. Some as we have seen in the programme "Long Lost Family" and other DNA programmes want to find their birth family and others don't. All in all, it is a personal decision and if you do want to look into your family history, I think you need to be prepared for the possibility of surprise. For me I didn't really know that much about my roots. I had grown up knowing my mother and little else. I was living with my mother and didn't know any other family member for many years. The norm is the norm until you discover it isn't and you discover the truth.

I signed up with Ancestry and started, as many of us do, looking into who my grandparents were where they originated from and where they had lived. I knew little about my mother's side of the family apart from that they came from Lincolnshire and some of the family had farms, but I didn't know much more than that. I knew from my mother that my maternal grandmother Susannah had lived with her and my dad in North Manchester towards the end of her life. My mother had said that she died when she was relatively young. When I obtained my grandmother's death certificate, I found out that she was only fifty-five years old when she passed. My mother was very close to her and was quite devasted when she became ill and died within a matter of a few months.

Apparently, my maternal grandfather, Walter, left his wife and children, my mother, and her brother Stan. I don't know why or even when. My mother didn't speak much about her father. I think she felt his desertion deeply and also the pain of her mother being deserted with two children. She had no time for her father and consequently I learnt nothing about him. After my grandfather's departure my grandmother went into service at a house as head cook for some Lord and Lady, so I am led to understand. I found out through my research that Walter was in the police and apparently a mounted policeman. My grandmother came from a large family of girls and was the eldest of seven. One story that my mother told me was my grandmother wrote to some person on a radio programme that she enjoyed, requesting a record to be played, 'Onward Christian Soldiers.' After weeks and weeks, it wasn't played. My grandmother was so disappointed, she stopped listening to the programme.

My father's family, the Winstanleys, at one time lived in close proximity to each other in Clayton, North Manchester. My mother, father and my maternal grandmother Susannah lived in one road and my father's two brothers Bill and Tom with their wives Nellie and Kath in an adjacent road. My paternal grandmother Caroline lived in a road round the corner. I guess my grandfather John James also lived there when the family came back from Malta. He was sixty-six when he died on 6th April 1941; I am told of sepsis. I never met him.

I was particularly interested in finding out about my father's side of the family as I knew relatively little about them. I didn't really know much about my mother's side of the family either but I thought I needed to start somewhere. I wanted to try and make sense of who my family were and find out their names. I had always been rather fascinated that my father's eldest brother Jim had the middle name of Abraham and wondered where that might have originated from. Like most people who start researching their family history I became more and more intrigued and fascinated. I found that my mother's relatives, as I had thought ,were from Lincolnshire and being able to join the dots and find family names made sense. It is interesting how names are passed down in families. I got side tracked at times, as one quite often does with research, but it was both enjoyable and fascinating at the same time.

For some reason that escapes me I decided to take a DNA test. I think it was due to some of my friends finding out where their ancestors had originated from. They were both intrigued and excited to learn even more about their family history. They would go and visit and explore the places where their ancestors had lived, especially in the British Isles. They often reported a feeling of warmth when visiting places that had family connections as if it was a place somehow known to them in some way.

My mother's side of the family were fair skinned with delicate and defined features. Apparently, they had descended from the Hugenots who had fled persecution and had come to England in the seventeenth century. My father's side of the family were mainly dark, especially on my grandmother's side, but my paternal grandfather was quite fair according to photographs I have seen of him. I was quite intrigued that my mother's side were very fair but my father's side were mainly dark. I was born with jet black curly hair which slowly changed into being a nondescript mousy colour. I would definitely prefer my black curly hair.

My DNA results arrived and to my utter surprise they revealed that I had an amazing number of Maltese relatives, from first cousins to fourth, fifth and sixth. I thought that it must be a mistake, an error of some kind and that it was absolutely incorrect. My father's family had lived in Malta for a number of years but, as far as I knew, that was that and I had no blood relatives who were actually Maltese. I ignored it. I continued to ignore it and I wondered how on earth it could be so wrong. I thought that somewhere along the line there had just been some sort of blip, a mistake, an error in the DNA processing and it was just a coincidence regarding Malta.

Citrus Fruit and Pomegranates

One day I was with a friend having a coffee and family research came up in conversation. I mentioned my DNA results. My friend said that I couldn't just ignore it because the DNA results wouldn't be incorrect they would be totally correct! I was very puzzled by the results and I still believed that there must be some sort of error somewhere. I have always believed in DNA as scientific proof but continued to think that, on this occasion, somehow there was an error and this was a coincidence. An odd one at that.

There were some fascinating Maltese names with my matches on the list I received from Ancestry, but I was still unconvinced these people were actually related to me.

I had by this time delved further into my mother's side of my family and confirmed they indeed descended through the French line of Hugenots who were French Protestants. They had travelled from France and had settled in and around Lincolnshire.

Then I chose to look into my paternal grandparents' side of the family as I was fascinated by the name of Abraham which ran through the family line. My uncle was James Abraham, my great grandfather was James Abraham and my great great grandfather was Abraham Winstanley. I wondered why Abraham had become a family name, then I also found Moses and Israel and other biblical names. I didn't ever find out why.

While I was quietly enjoying my research and finding out more information about my ancestors, Ancestry were advising me of more Maltese DNA Matches. More Maltese DNA connections were appearing on the list, I guess it was because more people were actually taking DNA tests. I was beginning to be intrigued but did nothing mainly because there was nothing I could do. I did wonder who these people might be? Why on earth were they showing up as my DNA Matches, my blood relatives?

One day I signed onto Ancestry and there was a message waiting for me from someone saying they thought we were related and that her mother was my cousin. Her mother was Maltese.

Four
Erbgha

The message in my inbox from Sarah said that she thought that she and her mother were relatives of mine and that her mother was, in fact, my cousin. How on earth could I have a Maltese cousin? How could this person's mother be my cousin? My mind went into overdrive, into a spin, and everything seemed to be jumbled in my brain. What on earth was going on? My father was far too young to have children of his own in Malta. He did have a family but those were his parents and siblings. He was about eight years old when he left and came to England so that wasn't the connection. None of his siblings would have been of an age to have children either. Nothing was making any sense to me.

Someone once told me that they thought my grandmother had lived in Malta as a child. If this was the case might this be the connection. I re-checked my grandmother's siblings on Ancestry and confirmed that her six siblings were in fact all born in the north of England.

Many years ago, I employed a Maltese genealogist to try and trace where my family lived whilst they were in Malta and also how long they lived there. Unfortunately, they weren't able to find any information. Attempts to find any records apparently failed. I had learned from my dad that the family had at one time lived in Valetta as well as Paola where he and his siblings were born. One of my cousins also told me that, when he went to Malta with his partner and his dad, my father's younger brother Tom, his dad (my uncle) tried to find where he and the family lived in Valletta. They did have the aid of a street map but seemingly where they lived had since been demolished, probably during the war. Malta was absolutely devastated during the second world war.

At one time I applied for a Maltese passport. Eventually, after months and months of phone calls and paperwork I decided to go to the offices in Malta in person whilst I was there. I was told that I was indeed eligible for a passport due to my father being born in Malta as he would be Maltese by birth. All the negotiations took a long long time and, by the time I was eventually allowed to have a passport, I had become somewhat disheartened by the whole ongoing drawn out process and I decided to leave it. I was getting nowhere with any of my research, my enquiries or genealogists.

When my father and his siblings were born Malta was a British Colony and therefore Maltese born people were British subjects. Malta gained independence from the United Kingdom on 21st September 1964.

I decided to undertake some research of my own at one time in the library in Valletta. I was only allowed in because fortunately I had a card with me saying that I was a Faculty Member of a University in England. It was quite difficult to get in for some reason, why I can't remember or maybe I didn't even know why. I was once again trying to trace where my family had lived but nothing came of that either. It was as though my family had never existed or had never even lived in Malta. It was as if my family of seven were totally invisible for some reason and it added to the ongoing frustration and mystery.

Now all this mystery was changing. I had someone contacting me saying they were a Maltese relative, in fact a Maltese cousin and I was thrown.

I was perplexed how come I had Maltese relatives? Now someone was making contact with me saying they thought we were related and not only that she thought her mother was my cousin. I was quite astounded. Ancestry indicated that I had Maltese relatives but I hadn't really taken it seriously. I thought it was a mistake. Why I don't know. Maybe I was in some sort of denial in some way. Now it seemed as if these DNA matches might prove to be correct after all and it was me who was wrong. I wondered what on earth was going on.

A friend wrote this in his letter to me. "The whole story of your family is complicated and I love the idea of you discovering relatives near and far. I can relate to you deciding that the DNA test was 'wrong'. Sometimes there can be too much truth, sometimes we just need to stay where we are for a moment and not have to cope with another change".

Sarah who initially contacted me regarding our DNA connection asked me over the following weeks and months what information I had about my family. We exchanged a good many emails with each other. Sarah was as intrigued as I was fascinated. Neither of us knew how we were related but she assured me that she was looking into it and intended to find out. We were both aware that neither the name Winstanley or the name Pewtress, my grandfather and grandmother's last names, were Maltese. Therefore, once again my family couldn't be Maltese. Could they?

According to the DNA matches I had quite a few Maltese relatives. Somehow. I also felt somewhere deep inside that this might well be true but nothing, absolutely nothing, had ever confirmed this. It was as they say, just a feeling. Again, that old record in my head asked me why did my father resemble people in Malta? Why was I mistaken for being Maltese? Could there possibly be more to this?

Over time I explained to my new found relation Sarah that I had no clue how I could have any Maltese relatives. I sent her various family documents including my father's birth certificate. I explained that my aunt and uncles were born in Malta; that the family lived there for a while and that my grandfather was a ships' engineer and worked in the dockyards in Malta.

Again, Sarah and I exchanged numerous emails and over the following weeks and months I learned that Sarah's mother was born in Paola. The same as my father. Obviously, there was quite an age difference as Sarah's mother is a similar age to me. But the same place what a coincidence it seemed to me at the time. In all the places in all the world!

After searching through even more documents and after more discussions and emails with each other Sarah advised me that the DNA matches I had alongside the measurement of Centimorgans and Segments indicated that I must definately have a Maltese grandparent. I knew that both Caroline, my grandmother, and John, my grandfather, were born in Lancashire in England. It just didn't fit.

Centimorgans apparently describe the length of DNA. They are a unit of genetic measurement measured to ascertain the connection with a relative or relatives in general. DNA segments are in all of the twenty-two chromosomes. Triangulated segments are segments that all DNA share with each other. Apparently, centimorgans might be more useful than DNA. It all seemed extremely precise specialized and scientific.

Now we were on the trail of my grandparents which would certainly make sense age wise. I knew my grandparents were married and had seven children, five of whom survived. My grandfather as I mentioned worked in shipyards in both England and Malta as an engine fitter. I am not sure whether he was in the Merchant or the Royal Navy or whether he was a civilian employed by the shipyards. It was by all accounts quite a specialized and important job. Maybe due to the type of work that he did he was away from my grandmother at times. Might he have had a relationship with someone whilst he was away? But if he did how would that have given me Maltese DNA?

Sarah was as intrigued as I was regarding all this. She kindly ran other comparison tests on another website between her mother and myself and it substantiated that there were indeed shared DNA matches. The test confirmed we were second or third cousins. As Sarah pointed out this was her family as well as mine and she wanted to get to the bottom of it as much as I did. She said that she was excited about the research and very much looking forward to sharing it with her mother. I was also excited and pleased to have someone to share all this with.

We were interested as to why my family were actually in Malta rather than anywhere else. Was it because as I had been told, that due to my grandmother's weak lungs, her doctor suggested she moved to a warmer climate? Was it my grandfather's work that took them to Malta? Was there a connection with another family member living there? Were there

Citrus Fruit and Pomegranates

relatives that we actually didn't know about? Apart from what my grandfather did for work and knowing that my grandparents' names weren't Maltese we were once again at a dead end and unfortunately it felt like we were getting nowhere. Well, apart from now knowing that I did actually have Maltese blood somehow.

My cousin Sheila, my Auntie Leta's daughter, had taken a DNA test previously to me, and her name showed up as a connection in our DNA matches. It indicated that we definitely matched but as a first or second cousins. Why first or second cousins surely she should be a first cousin as Leta was my dad's sister. An uncle or an aunt's child is a first cousin. Was this an indication of a different grandparent?

The DNA Match indicated another first or second cousin someone named Doris with a Maltese last name. I had never heard of Doris. The DNA also identified someone with the initials J.B. as another first or second cousin. Who on earth could this be? I thought I knew who all of my cousins were.

As I looked further at the records Ancestry stated, 'This is a preview of the public tree linked to J.B's DNA results. Surnames that appear in both your tree and J.B's tree are marked in green'. That didn't help me as there were no names marked in green. It then went on to say 'We can't find any common ancestors for you and J.B. This can happen if your Ancestry trees aren't linked to your DNA results, or if you don't have the same people in your trees. If we find any common ancestors for you and J.B., you'll be able to see them here'. It indicated that we were related through our DNA as first or second cousins but it wasn't apparent in either of our trees how we were related.

There was even more. There was someone named Margaret with a DNA match and Ancestry indicated she was also a second or third cousin of mine. Who was Margaret? I didn't know of a Margaret either. I ran the names of my cousins through my head and I couldn't identify her.

I was now totally and utterly perplexed. Perplexed I might be but it was now absolutely clear that I did have Maltese cousins. There was definitely a Maltese connection somehow and somewhere but the question was how and where? The how and where question seemed to be becoming my mantra alongside the old Johnny Nash song repeatedly going round and round in my head, "There are more questions than answers and the more I find out the less I know."

There was another second or third cousin identified with the last name of Mifsud which was definitely a Maltese name. Another second or third cousin was someone called Lola and Lola's tree was managed by a person with the last name of Borg. Sarah was also identified as a second or third cousin. There was also a Borg-Smith. All this seemed very clear, even if a little confusing as to who these people were. They were there though and Sarah and I were also there.

Then more and more names started to show up as second third or fourth cousins all with Maltese names. Names such as Attard, Aquilina, Bonello, Borg, Gauci, Camilleri, De Bono, Gauci, Pace, Azzopardi, Schembri. Names I didn't know and people I didn't know of who seemed to be my relatives. In fact there were loads of relatives and they were all Maltese.

As Sarah and I became more aquainted with each other she floated the idea had I ever considered my father Bert might be half Maltese because it seemed that that was what was being indicated. I actually hadn't even thought about it. Why would I even consider it? As far as I was concerned there was no reason to. My grandfather was born in Lancashire and he certainly wasn't Maltese.

The information in the next email I received from Sarah confirmed she had spent even more time comparing matches. She said she had a theory if I would like to hear it. She added that it might throw a curve ball into what I knew about my family but of course, like me, she was fascinated and wanted to help untangle the mystery. I said, "Yes absolutely throw me the curve ball." I was open to anything. The curve ball was that maybe it was my grandmother who had a relationship with someone and therefore John Winstanley wasn't my biological grandfather. Deep breath.

If I did have something like twenty two percent Maltese DNA, it would make me a quarter Maltese and my dad half Maltese. So, Sarah's theory, in fact the curve ball that Sarah sent asking if I had ever considered that my grandmother might have had a relationship with someone other than my grandfather seemed quite feasible. I hadn't considered that my grandmother might have had a relationship with someone other than my grandfather, or in fact someone who was Maltese. I had never thought about it. Why would I? Then I remembered the story of my mother saying to my grandmother that my dad didn't look English. My grandmother telling her to be quiet and to never mention it again. For some reason we hadn't taken the story that seriously or even given it much consideration as my grandmother, my aunt, my uncle Tom and my dad were all quite dark skinned and dark haired. My father was perhaps more so, slightly darker with a more olive tone to his skin. We just took for granted in a way that my dad didn't look English. It was just one of those things that we accepted. Perhaps he didn't look English because in fact he did have a Maltese father. Maybe my grandmother had had a relationship with a Maltese man. If so who could he possibly be? Who was my father's father? Who was my grandfather? Who was my grandmother's lover? Were they lovers? This was not what I had expected.

I was so grateful that someone was taking an interest in all of this with me. I was getting nowhere on my own and now someone was thinking about things and actually coming up with ideas and statistics. As much as all this was rather a surprise it was also a breath of fresh air.

Previously Sarah had undertaken a tremendous amount of research regarding her own family and her Family Tree. She kindly suggested that she sent me a copy of her Family Tree to have a look at. Sarah wanted to try and figure out who my biological grandfather might be. Me too! There was also information in her email about triangulating the amounts of DNA which I knew absolutely nothing about and also information looking at second cousin connections. Alongside this Sarah was looking at the DNA connections that we both shared and also working out how they matched which would take quite a while. In the meantime, I received Sarah's tree but there wasn't any obvious connection in the tree between her and my ancestors.

I must admit whilst all this was happening, I was going through a whole variety of emotions including astonishment, excitement, disbelief and bewilderment. I was both fascinated and pleased because all I had previously thought and believed was now unfolding. It was as if the pattern of the kaleidoscope was taking shape. Yet on another level I was deeply shocked by the whole situation.

I learned that first cousins share approximately 870 cm of DNA with one another and around 437cm is more than normal for second cousins. Sarah identified two second cousins that her mother and I shared with each other and she contacted both of them.

My DNA showed that my two English cousins shared 437cm and 504cm respectively meaning they must in fact be my second cousins rather than first my cousins. My Auntie Leta's daughter Sheila showed no Maltese DNA in her testing whatsoever. This would fit then with Sheila's grandfather being John Winstanley and my grandfather being someone other than John Winstanley.

There were two Maltese cousins shown in my DNA match and we had 413 cm and 365 cm. So, it seemed that my biological grandfather must in fact have been Maltese and my grandmother Caroline must have had a relationship with a Maltese man after all. We were now getting somewhere but in fact that somewhere was far from what I had ever imagined.

No wonder my dad looked Maltese and no wonder people thought that I was Maltese when in Malta. After all this information and all these years of research and wondering some of it was now starting to make sense. But who was this mystery man? Who on earth was my biological grandfather?

Then Sarah identified, through even further research, that the person in our DNA match with the initials J.B. was a cousin who lived in the States. J.B.

Citrus Fruit and Pomegranates

was both a match for Sarah, her mother Marlene and myself, but was actually more directly matched with me as a first or second cousin. We didn't quite know how or why, or even who they were.

The DNA match with Margaret proved that we were either second or third cousins which was the same as Sarah's mother Marlene and me. The DNA match also identified that Marlene and Margaret were second or third cousins. They were the descendants of two sisters, Emily and Elvira Borg. Apparently, Margaret was the grandaughter of Emily Borg and Marlene's great grandmother was Elvira. There was an age gap between Emily and Elvira due to them being from a large family, infact about fourteen years difference between them.

Emily and Elvira's parents we eventually found to be Carmelo and Carmela. Initially it seemed that they were both born in 1848. Later further research and documentation from Malta proved that Carmela was actually born four years earlier, in 1844. The question now seemed to be whether Carmela and Carmelo had any sons. Again, with more research we found out that they did. They were a family of eight children, three daughters and five sons. Might this in some way be the connection that we were looking for? Could one of Emily and Elvira's brothers actually be my biological grandfather?

Was J.B's grandfather my grandfather? It would make sense given the close connection with our DNA.

71

As I said previously, I had never thought about my grandmother having a relationship with anyone apart from my grandfather. Why would I have even have considered it, she was my grandmother after all. My father did look slightly different from his siblings but we had never questioned it that much until now. We know that not all siblings look alike and there can be differences in family resemblances dependent on the genes. Now we started looking at family photographs again and this time with different eyes. We could see the difference between my dad and his siblings. He had a different build and definitely had more of an olive skin and a darker skin tone with black hair that was much thicker and wavier.

I thought again of the conversation my mother had with my grandmother saying my dad didn't look English, and my grandmother telling my mother to be quiet and never mention it again. We certainly didn't give the story much thought at the time and assumed it was my grandmother telling my mother to be quiet because it was just one of those things. We hadn't taken it seriously. My grandmother quite obviously didn't want to talk about it because maybe my father's father wasn't English after all. Also, Wendy said as children they were told that my dad was dark because he was sun tanned! Now the pieces of the jigsaw were fitting together. Again, the question, if my biological grandfather was actually a Maltese man then who was he?

Five
Hamsa

We needed to ascertain some family history and needed to be absolutely certain that we had the correct parents for Emily and Elvira. Carmelo and Carmela did indeed fit. Initially, we found that Carmela was born Carmela Sant in approximately 1848 in Valletta, Malta. Since then church records have proven she was actually born Carmela Victoria Gudith Sant on 11th February 1844 in Naxxar. She married Carmelo Joseph John Enrico Dominic Borg on 4th October 1866 in Birkirkara Malta. Carmelo was born on 12th March 1848.

Carmela and Carmelo had four daughters and five sons. Might this give us a clue regarding my DNA match? We found that the girls were Elvira born in 1872, Caterina 1880, Emily 1886, and Maria in 1888.

Records show that Carmela and Carmelo's first son Alfred was born in 1872, Emanuel in 1874, Giuseppe (Joseph) in 1878, Edward in 1884, and then John but we haven't actually ascertained his date of birth.

The next step now was to see if all the male siblings survived and we were fortunate enough to find that they did and they all married but Giuseppe

(Joseph) seemed to have had two wives. So we needed to delve into this a little further.

Research and documentation showed Giuseppe was married to both Evellina and Helen. There was more to unravel and we needed to try and find out who he was actually married to out of these two women. Once again, we needed to find even more records.

Eventually, we found that Giuseppe (Joseph) and Evellina were married on 13th July 1897 in Pieta until Evellina's untimely death in 1911. She was only thirty-two. Evellina was born on 11th February 1879 and passed on 7th June 1911. During her short lifetime she had given birth to six children. Mary was born in 1898 and Edward the third child was born in 1902. They both survived but unfortunately the others were infant deaths. I have been told that Evellina died in child birth and also that she had Lupus.

In Malta at the time of Evellina's passing a child or children who had lost a parent had to be taken into care. Apparently, it was a decision taken by the church or the priest, so I have been informed. I am not sure whether it was actually the law at the time. If it was the law then the words of William Shakespeare come to mind, the law is an ass. Consequently, Mary aged thirteen and Edward aged eleven were both taken into care which must have been awful for them having already lost their mother and then being separated from their father. Awful too for Giuseppe (Joseph) losing his wife and then his two children being taken away.

Giuseppe went on to marry Helen on 7th January 1912 and they were allowed to have Mary and Edward home from care. They had several children together.

Their first child Evelyn and was born in 1914. John in 1915. Followed by Lillian and Elsie who sadly were infant deaths. Josephine was born in 1920, David in 1922, also an infant death and Valhmor in 1924.

The DNA Match showed that there was a connection somewhere with this family and it seemed that Giuseppe (Joseph) might just prove to be my biological grandfather.

My grandmother Caroline was born 6th December 1877 so she was of a similar age to the sons of Carmelo and Carmela and certainly a similar age to Giuseppe, although that doesn't automatically follow but it was worth looking into.

Looking back at the notes and according to Ancestry the DNA Matches I had both Doris as a first or second cousin and J.B. as my first or second cousin. Marlene and Margaret were second or third cousins.

We then found out that J.B. was Joan, the daughter of Edward the eldest son of Giuseppe and Evellina. If this was the link Giuseppe (Joseph) must in fact be my biological grandfather. There was no other reason why Joan could be my first or second cousin without our fathers being related and indeed brothers or half-brothers. It now seemed more likely that my grandmother Caroline had a child with Giuseppe and that child was my father.

If all this had felt somewhat of a bombshell so far, it now felt like an explosion. The research was fascinating but the emotion that went with all of this was overwhelming.

My grandmother and my grandfather married in England in December, 1899 and they had five children before the birth of my father in 1912. They had another son after my father, Tom who was born in September 1915. Records show that my grandfather John James returned to England shortly after Tom was born, in November 1915. He returned to the dockyard in Devonport before being transferred to Rosyth in Scotland. My grandmother and her children as civilians were unable to travel. Civilians were not allowed to travel during the First World War and therefore had to wait until the war was over to return to England. My Auntie Leta told me that my grandmother missed her family and wanted to return to England because of the war.

I was consumed with curiosity and questions. I wondered how my grandmother Caroline and Giuseppe (Joseph) might have met each other. I wondered if both my grandfather and my grandmother had met with Giuseppe and somehow they had both got to know him. Maybe they knew Giuseppe and Evellina, maybe they knew Giuseppe and Helen. Apparently, it was reported in The Times of Malta that Giuseppe and Helen often used to invite naval officers from the ships that were berthed in Msida Creek for tea and cocktail parties at their home on occassions.. What was the story of my grandmother and Giuseppe?

Maybe my grandfather was away for periods of time working on ships leaving my grandmother alone. Was she lonely?

Surely, Giuseppe would be full of grief having lost his wife in the June of 1911. Giuseppe married Helen in January 1912. My father was born at the beginning of July 1912. This was an awful lot to assimilate. So many thoughts and so many stories can go through your mind when you are trying to understand things and make sense of them, and also achieve some perspective.

Giuseppe was Catholic and my grandmother Protestant and married. Giuseppe would need to have been married and to a Catholic woman to have his children home from care. I am not dismissing Giuseppe and Helen's love for each other. I don't know their story. I don't know any of this story. I do know that people married for convenience and I do know it is possible to love more than one person.

Did Giuseppe know my grandmother was carrying his child? Did my grandmother know? Did my grandfather know? How different the world was in

1911 and 1912. I guess, if nothing else, my grandmother would certainly have known by seeing her son, my father, when he was born as he resembled Giuseppe. Did my dad ever know that John James wasn't his father? Who knew what and who didn't?

At this point and for my own understanding and clarification I decided to use the term grandfather for the man who was my grandfather, John James Winstanley and to use the Maltese name Nannu for my new found biological grandfather, Giuseppe Borg. It would help me to differentiate between the two men.

I didn't know my grandfather John and the only photographs I have of him are when he was older and he looked quite fair. I don't know if this was the case or whether it was because he was older and his hair was grey. I think Jim, my dad's eldest brother might have been fair. I was fortunate enough to be given a photograph of uncle Bill recently by his granddaughter and it shows him to be quite dark when he was young. My grandmother was quite dark and so were my aunt Leta and my uncle Tom. My dad was even darker than his siblings and I became aware that this was because he resembled his father, Giuseppe. I apparently also resemble Giuseppe, so I am told.

Six
Sitta

Over the following months it transpired that Sarah, Marlene, Margaret and I developed a connection and friendship with each other that has proved to be quite special.

At some stage I found J.B. to be living in the States and I was given her phone number. Unfortunately, I cannot recall how I obtained her number but then so much has happened. I was advised by a friend to buy an international phone card and to make a call to her. I bought the phone card and with some anxiety, a certain amount of trepidation and maybe a glass of wine or two, I made the call.

The phone was answered by a soft American female voice which said "Hallo, is that my cousin?" I was so shocked and overcome that I don't really recall what my response was. I know I felt emotional that someone who I had never met and who lived on the other side of the world answered in such a way. I think I might have muttered something like, "Are we cousins?" Joan replied that we were indeed cousins because her father and my father were brothers and we shared the same grandfather, Giuseppe (Joseph) Borg. Bingo! So that was that so to speak, it was confirmed. I was stunned. It seemed it was now signed sealed and delivered. My biological grandfather was indeed Giuseppe Borg. This was my biological family and Joan was my second cousin because we actually shared the same grandfather and he was Maltese.

Over the years Joan had carried out an amazing amount of family research and had traced the Borg family back as far as the 1600's. She had also drawn the family tree by hand back to the 1600's which is very impressive. We talked for over an hour and a half on the phone. She gave me an incredible amount of family history and explained who was who in the family. She told me that she had a sister Judy who would be another cousin of mine. Judy was younger than Joan and lived on the West Coast in Washington. Joan and Judy also had had two brothers, Joseph and James who had both sadly passed away. We have had many wonderful conversations since then. Joan has been extremely kind in sharing information with me and telling me stories about our grandfather (Nannu) Giuseppe and great-grandfather, Carmelo, the family, and our mutual cousins. Through these stories I felt as though I came to know them.

Over the next few weeks and months letters and photographs from Joan began popping through my letterbox with little notes and explanations of who was who accompanying them. Then one morning the doorbell rang and there to my surprise was a second postal delivery of the day. The delivery person was standing there with a large off-white envelope in her hand. The envelope was from the States and as she handed me the envelope, she said with a smile, 'Enjoy your day!' I thought it was unusual to have two postal deliveries in one day. I thanked her very much and went inside to open the envelope which I recognized to be from the States and by the handwriting from Joan.

Neatly folded inside the off-white large envelope was copy of the family tree that Joan had researched and drawn up, by hand, the one she had patiently researched and had traced the family back to the 1600's. I stood there looking at all the names totally amazed with tears in my eyes. I was so moved by her thoughtfulness and by her generosity in sending it to me. I looked at the places these people had lived and I recognised some of the names of the people on the tree that I was related to. That evening I called Joan to thank her and to tell her how moved I was. She said that I was very welcome and she thought I should know who my ancestors were. What a gift.

In the meantime Sarah had contacted Margaret to ask if it was okay to forward her email address to me. Margaret immediately agreed and she was delighted to make contact with another member of the family. After all we had we had our Borg ancestry to share and discuss with each other.

Over the following months Margaret and I exchanged stories with each other and alongside the stories we exchanged family photographs. I was delighted to receive a photograph of Margaret's grandmother, Emily. Emily was Giuseppe's sister, my Nannu's sister. Emily was therefore my great-aunt. It was so good to see a photograph of Giuseppe's sister and to observe the likeness. Margaret also sent me a photograph of her parents. Margaret's father Joseph had been in the Maltese Navy and met Margaret's mother Mary whilst he was in England. When the time came, he left the Navy, left his homeland, married Mary and stayed in England. Mary and Joseph had three children, Kevin, Joseph and Margaret. Mary and Joseph were married for fifty-two years and lived in the North-East of England.

Both my father and Margaret's father lived in the North of England and they had no knowledge of each other nor of their family connection. Margaret and I have often spoken about how wonderful it would have been for them to have met and to have been able to share their stories with each other.

Since our initial contact and due to the Covid lockdown, we haven't at the time of writing been able to meet with each other but we hope to be able to rectify that very soon. We have shared much of our Borg family history and Maltese heritage, and have emailed each other with regularity for over a year now. Recently, we had our first Skype session and it felt as if we had always known each other. We have also noted our similarities and it was a lot of fun chatting and catching with each other.

Marlene and I are in frequent contact with emails and messages and we have also had a few Zoom sessions. We have smiled at our similarity in looks and on one occasion Sarah, Marlene's daughter, took a photograph of the three of us whilst on a Zoom session because of our resemblance. As with Margaret, we can chat endlessly. The time goes so quickly and as Marlene said it is as if we have known each other forever. She has been kind enough to invite me to stay with her in Malta. Marlene has property there although she has lived in England for many years.

Marlene and I have exchanged stories and photographs with each other. We have looked at some old family documents, some of which Marlene found whilst researching in Malta. For some reason many of the photographs I have taken whilst in Malta are of Maltese doors. The doors are large, rather grand and rather splendid. They fascinate me. I do wonder about the stories behind these doors.

On one occasion when Marlene visited Malta, she was kind enough to buy me two replicas of Maltese ornamental doors and posted them to me. One is now on the fridge and the other on the bookcase. When I look at them, I think what a lovely and kind gesture it was and I am grateful for both her thoughtfulness and generosity.

The actual order of events in getting to know my Maltese relatives escapes me at times because I was so totally overwhelmed. There was so much information to process and absorb and occasionally I wondered if it was real or in fact a dream. Was I really part of this family?

The mystery of my father's identity and my own identity was now becoming clear. These were the people with whom I shared and inherited my genetics, they were both warm and friendly just like my father and they were people I hadn't known anything about until now. They were surprisingly accepting that we were related and that we were family. They said that DNA doesn't lie and that apart from any thing else we all resembled each other in looks.

I needed to take the time to absorb that this side of my family were Maltese. That my father's father was Maltese. That my Nannu was Maltese. I needed to process this and reflect.

Joan shared with me the addresses of a few cousins and suggested I made contact with them. One of the cousins that I wrote to was Lucienne who lives in Malta. Maya, Lucienne's daughter contacted me the very same day that her mother received my letter and asked if I would contact her Mum on Messenger. I have to admit at the time I hadn't used Messenger and I wasn't familiar with it. The letter I sent to Lucienne arrived on a Tuesday. On the Saturday Lucienne called me. I was both surprised and delighted. We chatted for an hour and a half and again, as with Marlene and Margaret, we could have chatted for even longer. Since then, we have spoken much more and Lucienne has kindly sent me many family photographs. With stories and explanations of who is who in the family. As expected, it was confirmed that Lucienne and her two sisters and I share the same Nannu.

Apparently, Lucienne and her sister Therese were both surprised and shocked when they first saw photographs of my dad that I sent to them. Therese thought the photographs were of Giuseppe (Nannu) when he was a young man. So much is the likeness of my father to his father.

On another occassion I received a photograph of Giuseppe, which I had put on the mantlepiece in one of the rooms at home. One of my friends said what a good photograph it was of my dad. I told them it wasn't my dad to which my friend replied, 'I remember him looking like that.' Again, I said it wasn't my dad and my friend asked who it was if it wasn't my dad. I told her that apparently, it was my Dad's biological father who was Maltese. She was amazed by the resemblance and the story.

I also wrote to one other cousin in Malta. Joan had given me her name and address and suggested I contacted her, which I did twice. Unfortunately, she didn't respond. I was disappointed especially after the warm reception I had received from all the other family members up until now.

My next introduction to a cousin was to Joan's sister Judy, who lives on the West Coast of America.

She was really delighted to make contact with me and again we have exchanged many emails, stories and photographs.

Judy told me that she had put a photograph of my dad next to her dad in the family photos she has on the wall in her home. She said that the brothers should be together. I thought this was rather special. Judy posted on Facebook that I was a new found cousin and publicly welcomed me into the family, which was kind and generous. I was very touched.

More photographs and more stories. Judy sent me some photographs of her and Joan when they visited Malta. They were in Msida outside what I had learned to be Nannu's house. It was special for them visiting their Nannu's house and also for me receiving the photographs. Nannu had died many years before and the house had changed hands but it was wonderful for them to be able to travel from America to Malta and to be with family and visit the house.

By now I was in regular contact with my Maltese family. One day some months later and quite out of the blue I received an email from Ancestry saying there was a new DNA match for me. I must admit it was rather a surprise after all this time especially when I thought all my surprises had just about exceeded themselves.

This match didn't have a Maltese name and I couldn't place them. Of course, I realised at one time

I hadn't known any of my other DNA matches either. I decided to follow it up and it was indeed another Maltese connection. I contacted Brenda and I asked if she knew how we might be related. I quickly received a reply saying she didn't know and that she had looked at my family tree on Ancestry and couldn't see any connection whatsoever, between us.

By now, I had come to terms with the story of my grandmother, Caroline and Giuseppe. I decided to email Brenda and explain. I told her the story of my grandmother and Giuseppe. Giuseppe and Brenda's grandmother Mary were brother and sister. We now had Elvira, Emily, Giuseppe and Mary placed and photographs of three of them.

Brenda was initially interested in researching her mother's side of the family when our DNA Match popped up on Ancestry. Our connection with each other was spontaneous and immediate.

Brenda knew her great grandparents were Carmelo and Carmela Borg and I was pleased to be able to forward photographs of them both to her. Photographs that Joan had initially sent to me. We enthusiastically shared our stories of who was who and where and how people fitted into the family. I was delighted to receive photographs from Brenda of her immediate family and especially a photograph of her grandmother Mary. It was fascinating to see the similarity between Mary and Giuseppe.

Brenda was very interested in my story and how I had actually found out about my Nannu. When she did see the photographs of my dad and of me she said she could really see the Borg resemblance. She also put photographs of Giuseppe, my dad, and myself together as a photographic comparison and sent them to me. I appreciated it and by now, as I said, I had come to terms with being part of this Borg family. I was proud of my roots and connections. I must admit there was some relief knowing the truth and a sense of satisfaction.

Brenda lives in Australia and we have emailed each other now with some regularity. We had our first Skype session which lasted two and a half hours. Time went very quickly as it had with both Marlene and Margaret when we spoke. It was as if we had always known each other and I guess in some way we have.

It is amazing how much research we can carry out on the World Wide Web. It's wonderful emails can be so spontaneous and how amazing Skype and Zoom are. They give us the ability to connect more or less immediately with people around the world. It has given us the ability to connect with people that we wouldn't have been able to connect with, due to a world where travel has been curtailed by a virus.

I guess technology has brought my family together. We were separate links in a chain and now we are joined together. It is strange to think that I share my genetics with all these family members,

Citrus Fruit and Pomegranates

especially, as I didn't know about them until two years ago. So much has happened in those two years.

Seven
Sebgha

I thought I had learned all there was for me to learn regarding my new family. Brenda however, informed me that her father, Alfred had written some notes about the Borg family. She thought that her brother Joe had them and said she would check with him the following day.

Brenda spoke with Joe and within a matter of days I received an email with a PDF document attached which was ten pages of A4 paper with the title, 'Borg our Ancestors'. By Alfred Psaila. Underneath the title was a photograph of the Roman Catholic Baroque church in Msida, which is Saint Joseph's Parish Church. To the right-hand side of the church was Giuseppe's house. Nannu's house. Many years ago, I had stood looking at this house not realising the connection.

When Brenda made contact she always referred to Giuseppe as my Grandfather or my Nannu. It felt inclusive and warm and friendly. As I write my story I feel as though I have bonded with my Nannu. It is as if I have got to know him through my cousins including me, the stories they have shared with me and their generous contributions.

Brenda took the trouble of typing up her father's notes which she kindly sent to each of us. We were delighted. It was as if our relatives had come to life. How very grateful we are to Alfred (Borg) Psaila for taking the trouble and time writing these notes and also to Brenda. It has allowed us to learn so much more about our aunts and uncles and our great-grandfather, Carmelo. It has been such a gift getting to know each other and these notes were certainly an added bonus.

In the days that followed I learned that Nannu had a house on the left-hand side of St Joseph's Church in Msida before he had the property on the right-hand side of the church. He went on to obtain another property known as the Grand Hotel and by all accounts he moved into the hotel and lived there until his death on 21st April 1957. Nannu was born and died on the 21st April. He was was seventy-nine years old. My father Bert, was born on 2nd July and died on 2nd July, when he was seventy-nine years old.

As we had already identified Nannu was indeed married twice and his first wife Evellina died when she was quite young. Their children Mary and Edward survived. They also had four children who unfortunately didn't survive Emily, Guzi, Guza and Amy. I want to include them in this story and to name them because so doing it is to honour them.

As I said earlier it certainly took some investigative research to find out that Nannu had been married twice. Initially, I thought the records must be incorrect in some way. His second wife was Helen and they had several children together, Evelyn, John, Lillian, Elsie, Josephine, David, and Valhmor. Lillian and Elsie were both infant deaths and again I want to include and acknowledge them in this story.

Nannu's two marriages were eventually confirmed for me by Joan before we aquired any documentation.

Evellina's untimely death was on 7th June 1911 and Giuseppe married Helen on 7th January 1912. My father was born at the beginning of July, 1912.

At the time my father was born my grandmother Caroline and my grandfather John James were married. I will never know the story of my grandmother, my grandfather and my Nannu.

I wonder what my grandmother and my Nannu's story was and how my grandfather John James fits into this. I am curious as to whether Nannu knew that my dad was his son and whether my Dad and Nannu ever had any contact with each other. I guess unless Nannu and my grandmother stopped seeing each other he must have had some idea Bert was his son, apart from anything else he looked so very much like him.

Did my grandfather and my Nannu actually know each other, and did my dad ever know that John James wasn't his biological father? Did Giuseppe and Caroline keep in touch with each other after the birth of my father or even after she returned to England? Did anyone know their story and if so, who knew?

My dad left Malta and came to England when he was about eight years old, I believe. He left with his mother and his four siblings. It would have been after the end of the the First World War around 1920. Civilians were not allowed to travel during the war. According to my grandfather's records he returned to England in 1915 and went directly to Devonport in Plymouth and then on to Rosyth in 1916. He was discharged in October 1917 at his request.

I was nine when Nannu died in Pieta, Malta 21st April, 1957. He was seventy-nine. Caroline died the year before on 28th June, 1956 in Ashton Under Lyne, Lancashire, England. She was seventy-eight.

Eight
Tmienja

When I was eleven and discovered that Mike wasn't my dad and my dad was Bert Winstanley who I thought to be my uncle, it took some adjusting to. But as I had been close with him as my uncle, I became much closer to him as my dad.

My friends who met my dad over time remarked how much we were alike. We had the same mannerisms and, to the irritation of my mother, the same sense of humour.

My world as a child was isolated and lonely. Until I was about eleven years old the only relative I really knew was my mother. It didn't make sense as a child that my uncle Bert was a relative because he wasn't my mother's brother.

When I eventually spent time with my dad I was fascinated, watching him and seeing similar movements and mannerisms as me was quite strange. Here was someone I was actually like. Someone I looked like, moved like and laughed like. On a deep level I just knew him and it was so easy.

I wasn't aware of watching Leta or Tom in the same way. Bill was quite unwell and on an oxygen cylinder due to a collapsed lung through asbestos poisoning at work. When I visited him he was usually sitting down because he was so weak. It felt quite warming that these people were my dad's sister and brothers, my aunt and uncles and therefore blood relations.

I remember at my dad's funeral people were sitting around outside the crematorium when I arrived. I didn't know who these people were or whether they were relations or friends of my dad's. I was asked who I was. The whole thing was surreal and it felt as though I had lost my dad for the second time.

Alongside all of this I wondered whether my dad's other daughter, my sister was there. I wouldn't know who she was. I always felt that I had a sister and at night I used to dream that I travelled to her house which I thought to be in America. I always had the initial 'A' in the dream. I grew up in a time when America was prominent in the news and on the television and we were impressed with all things American. Imagine how I felt when I learnt about astral travelling. My sister had lived in Australia for a period of time.

I guess we adjust. After my dad had passed, I continued to go to Manchester to visit my aunt and uncle.

When I looked at the Winstanleys there was a resemblance but, when the story of the Borgs first unfolded and I started seeing photographs, the resemblance was incredible. Here were people that I really did look like.

My dad definitely looked like his father Giuseppe and I resemble both of them. I also looked like my Maltese cousins. My cousin Joan sent me a photograph of one of our uncle's who would be one of my dad's brothers. He and my dad looked very alike it shocked me to my core. Also I looked so much like him, an uncle that I never knew, in fact never even knew of until recently. Friends seeing the photograph of him have asked if he was my dad!

As I got to know more of my Maltese family and gathered cousins, we discussed the resemblance we had to each other. We also enjoyed the same sense of humour. They showed a warmth and acceptance that was new to me and we continue to keep in touch.

How do I explain the closeness and warmth I felt for my father when I believed him to be my uncle? I guess somewhere deep inside I must have known that he was my dad.

How do I explain the feeling I had about having a sister? It was something in the depth of me, a sort of knowing.

Much, much more why did tears uncontrollably run down my face when the plane descended into the airport on my first ever visit to Malta? This was long before I knew about my Maltese family background and long before I knew about my genetics.

How come I always felt at home in Malta, as if I belonged there? At one time I thought it was because my dad and his brothers and sister were born there and that my grandparents and the family had lived there.

I now understand why I feel so at home in Malta and why my dad looked Maltese. Why I am taken for being Maltese when I am in Malta. I used to say when asked, 'No, I'm not Maltese'. Next time I'm there and I am asked whether I am Maltese, I will have a very different answer.

It is more than that and now I know.

Linda Borg-Winstanley

Bert Winstanley

2nd July 1912 – 2nd July 1991

Always known as Bert. This was my dad. When I was young and didn't really know him that well I asked someone what he was like. Their reply was that he was the kindest person they knew. I guess that sums it up.

Citrus Fruit and Pomegranates

Caroline Pewtress

6th December 1877 – 28th June 1956

Caroline, Pewtress was my grandmother, I know little about her. She was born on 6th December 1877 in Bradford, Manchester which is in the north of England.

Her parents were Mary Ann Heap and George Pewtress. Caroline was the eldest of seven children and was followed by James, Mary, George, Eliza, Elizabeth and Sarah.

Mary and George lived in the countryside in Herefordshire and George was an agricultural worker, until like many people at the time, he had to move to the north of England for work. George became a coal miner.

Caroline married my grandfather John James Winstanley when she was twenty two and became Caroline Winstanley. She moved to Malta with John James and they lived in Malta for many years.

Caroline gave birth to seven children, six being children of my grandfather John James and one being the son of Giuseppe Borg. The children were Jim, George, Robert, Leta, Bill, Bert and Tom. Bert was the son of Giuseppe. Jim and George were born in England and the other children were all born in Malta.

My grandmother returned to England after the end of the first world war with her five children. Her husband apparently returned earlier due to his work in the Dockyards.

When Caroline returned to England she returned to the north and lived in close proximity to her children. I remember visiting her when I was young and I always felt a warmth and a connection. My memory tells me the house was quite dark, or the furniture was quite dark. Over the years I have come to realise that it had a sense of Malta about it.

Towards the end of her life Caroline lived with her daughter in Ashton Under Lyne and that is where she died at Leta's house on 28th June 1956.

Linda Borg-Winstanley

John James Winstanley

27th April 1875 – 6th April 1941

John James Winstanley was my grandfather and this is the only photograph I have ever seen of him. Every document I have ever come across always refers to him as John James, never just John, so John James it will be.

He was born in Blackburn Lancashire on 27th April 1875 and was one of four children. Emma, John

James, Herbert Guy and Phoebe, to parents James Abraham and Elizabeth Guy.

Records show that he was an iron turner before he became a ships engineer or an engine fitter or even both in England and then in Malta. When I contacted the National Archives to try and ascertain whether he may have been in the Navy, either the Merchant or Royal, they informed me that he would have been in one of them as he requested a discharge whilst in Rosyth, in 1917. We haven't to date been able to locate any documentation that might clarify the situation.

My grandfather had six children with my grandmother, five who survived. He brought up and provided for the surviving children and also my father Bert, whose biological father was Giuseppe Borg.

My grandfather died aged sixty six in Ancoats Hospital, Manchester on 6th April 1941, of Sepsis.

Linda Borg-Winstanley

Giuseppe Maria Borg
21st April 1878 – 21st April 1957

Citrus Fruit and Pomegranates

My biological grandfather Giuseppe was born on 21st April 1878 in Sliema, Malta.

I understand that he was educated at a private school on Gozo but at this point in time I don't know much more than that.

He was married twice, firstly to Evellina Maistre who died on 7th June 1911 and then to Helen Grixti on 7th January 1912.

As an adult Giuseppe was quite weathly and owned a company called, 'Marsa Cold Storage.' The company supplied ice to the whole of Malta and was the only company of its kind on the Island. He was known to be honest in his dealings and approachable. Like his father, Carmelo he was well thought of and well respected. He served the community of Msida as their Mayor.

Giuseppe lived in a grand waterfront house in Msida where he entertained his many international business and celebrity connections. He and Helen used to regularly invite visiting celebrities and senior British Naval Officers from various ships to the house for tea or cocktails and these events made regular news in the social pages of the Malta Times.

In his later years Giuseppe bought the Grand Hotel and lived in the hotel until his death on 21st April 1957. He suffered from type one diabetes and was looked after by Nino who worked for him, and had been his driver and right hand man. He looked after Giuseppe until his death.

Giuseppe remained generous until the end and his daughters in law said of him that he was the most esteemed person they knew.

He was laid to rest in the Borg grave East B- 21 Addolorata Cemetery, Paolo and was later moved to an adjacent grave with his second wife Helen and their family.

Carmelo Borg

12th March 1848 - 1928

My great grandfather Carmelo Joseph John Enrico Dominic Borg was born on the 12th March 1848 in Valletta. He had soft blue eyes and by all accounts was a very elegant man who enjoyed talking with all sorts of people regardless of who or what their station in life. Apparently, he was highly thought of and well respected.

Carmelo and Carmela during their lifetime together had nine surviving children.

Carmelo was always smartly dressed and liked to wear a starched white drill shirt, carry a cane with a silver knob and carry a gladstone bag with him, especially when he went to the market to shop which he enjoyed. He had lots of pairs of shoes which he liked to polish himself although he had servants. There was also a groom who would take care of his stabled horses.

Carmelo very much enjoyed Italian Opera and after preparing himself for about two hours would regularly travel in his horse and carriage to the Royal Opera House in Valletta.

With my great-grandparents being very well off, they owned a large house in Pieta before moving to an even larger house in Msida. The house, so I am told, had fourteen rooms, a large garden with a big pond, stables for the horses and tennis courts. There was also an abundance of orange and lemon trees.

In the evening the family would gather in the large courtyard which was called 'Circular'. It was full of flower pots and many beautiful flowers including jasmine. There were bunches of grapes hanging down from the vines. The table would always be full of various salads and wines.

Other rooms in the house were used for storage mainly for equipment used for Carmelo's commercial laundry business. He had a contract with the P&O Shipping Lines for both his commercial laundries and also the boats that used to come into Msida Creek which was very near to the house.

Carmelo lived until the age of eighty-three and was laid to rest in the Borg family grave East-B-21 at the Addolorata Cemetery in Paola with his wife Carmela, some children and many grandchildren.

In the words of his grandson, Alfred, "Grandpapa was the kindest, most affable gentle and down to earth person".

Citrus Fruit and Pomegranates

Carmela Borg

11th February 1844 – 11th June 1915

Linda Borg-Winstanley

Carmela Borg was my great grandmother. She was born Carmela Victoria Gudith Sant and born on 11th February 1844 in Naxxar.

She married Carmelo Borg on 4th October 1866 in Birkirkara when she was twenty two years of age.

We have recently discovered that Carmela had an older sister Paula who was born on 31st October 1841.

We also know that Carmela and Carmelo had nine surviving children during their life time together.

Unfortunately, we have little more information than that which is a shame because she must have been more than a daughter, wife, mother and grandmother.

Hopefully, our continuing research will help us glean more knowledge about Carmela Sant Borg and we will be able to give her the recognition she deserves within the family.

Carmela died aged seventy-one years of age on 11th June 1915 and was buried in the Borg family grave East-B-21 at the Addolorata Cemetery, Paola.

Citrus Fruit and Pomegranates

Jim

Leta

Bill

Bert

Citrus Fruit and Pomegranates

Tom

Bill, Bert and Tom

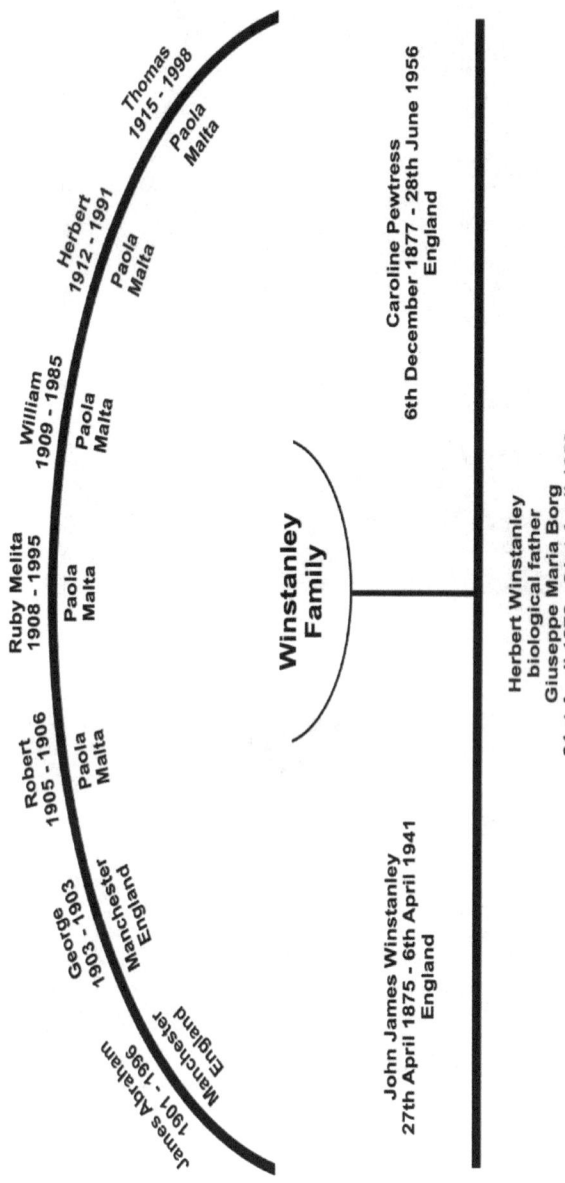

Citrus Fruit and Pomegranates

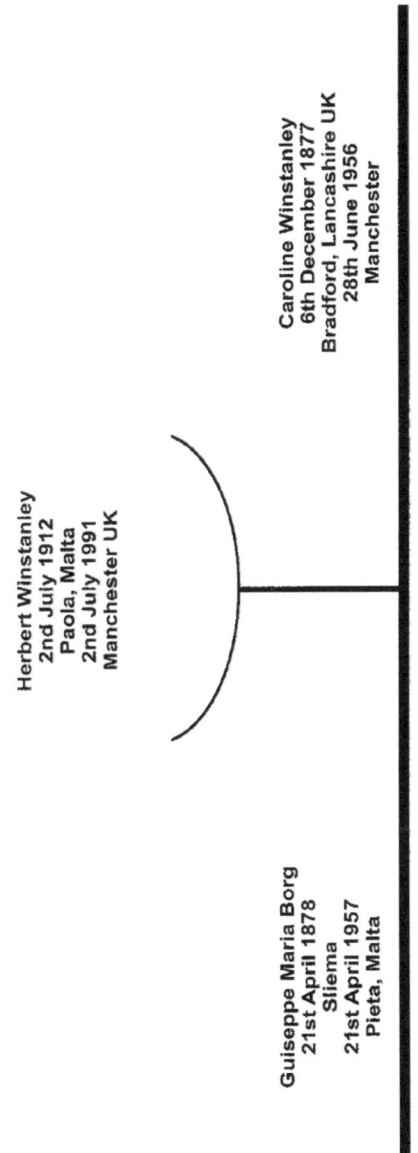

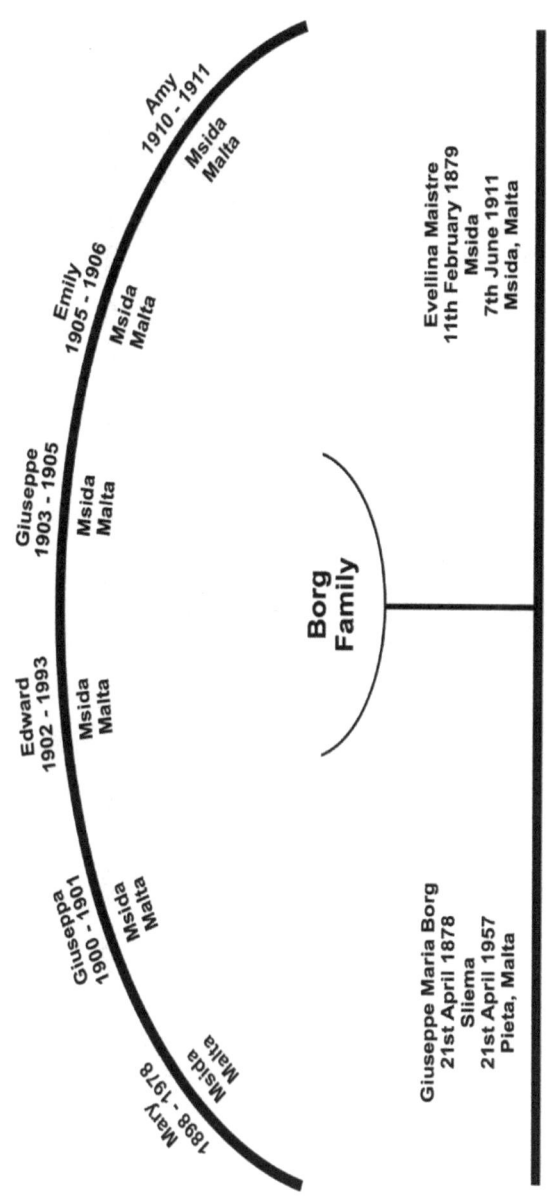

Citrus Fruit and Pomegranates

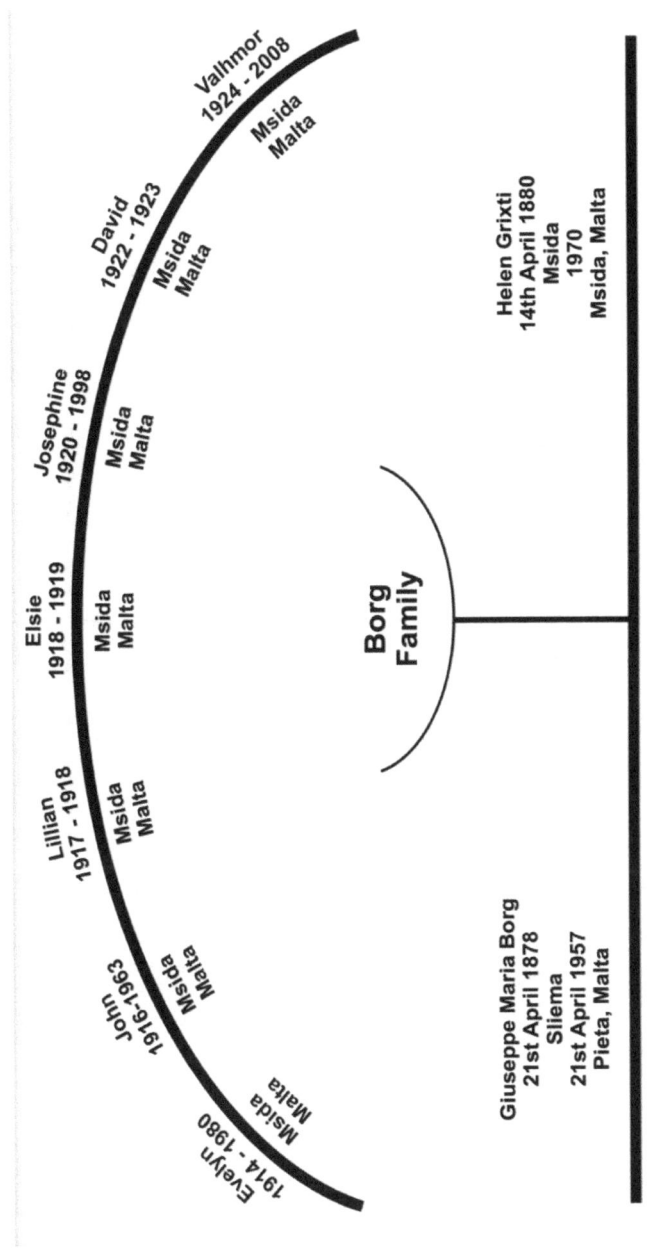

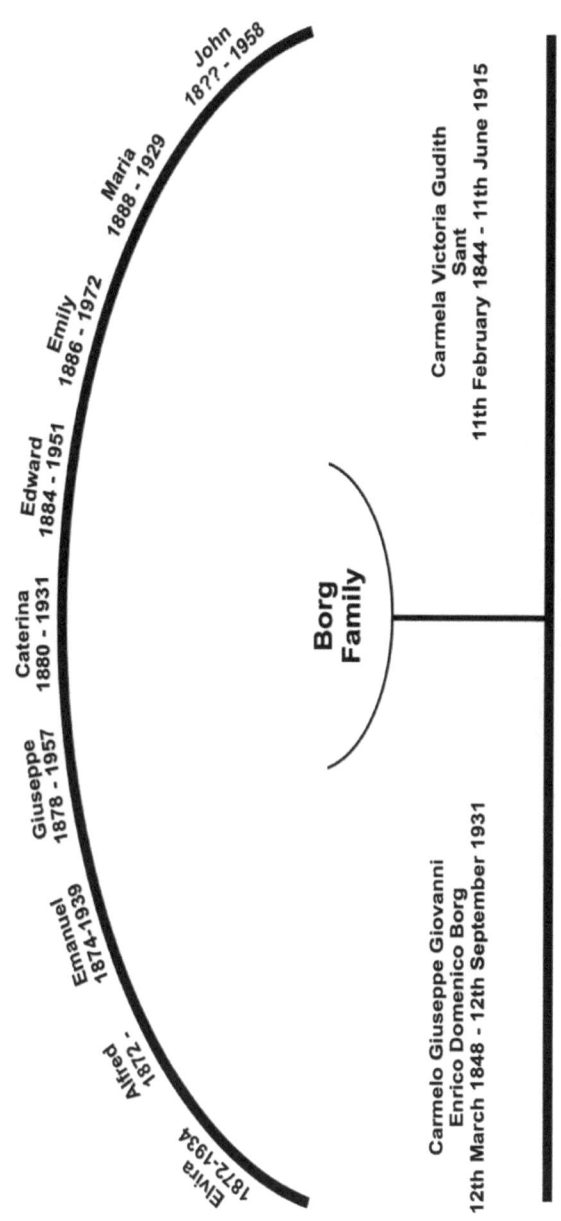

Acknowledgements

My sincere appreciation firstly to Sarah Bowen who was instrumental in my journey and changed my life without knowing it.

To all my Maltese cousins who have warmly accepted me as a member of the family and shared many stories and photographs with me. They are Marlene Leach, JoAn Borg-Bitton, Margaret Emmerson, Lucienne Bonello, Judy Borg-Talik, and Brenda Reed. Also, to Maya Bonello for her initial contact.

To Jean Bell, who listened and discussed my thoughts and meanderings with me which helped as she not only knew my dad but also danced with him.

Carol Ryan who read my words and tirelessly, encouraged me and made suggestions. To my old friend Linda Hisgett who also read through my words towards completion and also made suggestions.

To Anita Hart for kindly sending me a photograph of her grandfather, my uncle Bill, so I could complete the photo gallery.

Thanks to Fred and June Flanagan for their support and enthusiasm.

To Donna Akhtar for discussing the importance of lineage and family history. Lucy Brisbane for her kindness and endless emails regarding publishing. To Viv Courtney-Brisbane for reminding me you cannot ignore D.N.A.

To Nicholas Lee for the conversations and letters whilst writing my story.

Janiice Rider for her constant encouragement.

Wendy Sloane who like a sister has been there always, knowing my dad and understanding what Malta meant to me. Even when we didn't know.

To my cousin Tony Winstanley for the chats about the family and our grandfather.

Adrian Saker for adjusting photographs.

Frances Anderson for her invaluable help

Kully Bath for her enthusiasm and enormous help.

Rob Halliday-Stein for being him and for his help and encouragment.

Brian Durkin for always being there.

To Rosi who has tirelessly supported me with this journey and my life.

Also, a thank you that I cannot say in person to my dad and my grandmother who have in one way gone and in another way are still here.

BV - #0022 - 191223 - C0 - 203/127/7 - PB - 9781915657497 - Gloss Lamination